REX HUNT'S
FISHING

Adventures
and
Fact Book

IRONBARK
Pan Macmillan Australia

First published 1995 in Ironbark by Pan Macmillan Australia Pty Limited
St Martins Tower, 31 Market Street, Sydney

National Library of Australia
cataloguing-in-publication data:

Hunt, Rex.
Rex Hunt's fishing adventures and fact book

ISBN 0 330 35729 8.

1. Hunt, Rex. 2. Fishing - Australia. 3. Fishing - Australia - Anecdotes.
I. Title. II. Title : Fishing adventures and fact book.

799.10994

Typeset in 12/14 pt Bembo
Printed by Australian Print Group, Maryborough, Vic.

Technical drawings by Geoff Wilson.
Cartoons by Scott Rigney.

Every attempt has been made to source the photographs included in this book. Publishers that may have been
inadvertently overlooked should contact the publisher.

I dedicate this book to my wife Lynne, and our children Matthew and Rachel.

CONTENTS

A MESSAGE FROM REX HUNT

I feel honoured to have been accepted by so many anglers of this country, to represent you in the field of fishing.

I have no doubt that since the inception of 'Rex Hunt's Fishing Adventures', thousands of people have discovered the wonderful world of recreational fishing.

With the assistance of our team many people are learning the skills of fishing.

I am pleased that I no longer measure my success on the water by the amount of dead fish lying at the bottom of the boat or alongside me on a river bank.

I have been fortunate in travelling Australia and in fact the world in my capacity as a television fishing presenter. I have watched as people on my team have become household names to the viewers of the show.

It has been satisfying also that we now have heroes in our beloved sport of fishing. Not necessarily the best anglers in Australia but people who have the ability to deliver a style that is enjoyed and understood by all, but more importantly representing mainstream Australia.

However, all things come at a cost. Many of us spend far too much time away from our homes and families.

The most sobering thing is the responsibility that goes with such a position. I am delighted to see the 'Catch, kiss and release' campaign growing every day.

We, the recreational anglers of this country, have a long battle ahead of us. We must demand a fairer deal. We must stop those people who in the name of 'making a quid' destroy fish habitats and kill thousands of unwanted fish.

Unfortunately we must also give a loud and clear message to those in our ranks who abuse the resource through greed, that no longer will this be tolerated in modern times.

We must all show restraint in the amount of fish we catch. A well worn phrase says it all. Limit your catch, don't catch your limit.

Perhaps the most important thing of all is the kids. My thoughts have not changed since I was a kid. If you place a fishing rod in the hands of a kid you are doing him a great favour. That kid will not only learn about fishing, he will respect the environment we live in and meet a wide range of people from all walks of life along the way, fishing is a great leveller.

My message to every kid who reads this is clear. Reach for the stars, the sky is the limit. Dream, dream big, dream long and above all live that dream. A seven year old kid in 1956 caught his first fish, he has been dreaming ever since.

It is probably not fair to single out people who have assisted me along the way. There have, quite bluntly, been hundreds of people who have helped and assisted me, some without even knowing it.

However, I would like to mention the following people who have been instrumental in me reaching this stage. Special thanks to: Jim Allen, Kaj Busch (Bushy), Mike Dickinson (Producer), John Dumphy (Shimano Australia), Bob Grieve (Associate Producer), Don Hyde (My Publisher), Paul B. Kidd, Greg Numa (My Manager) and Steve Starling.

And of course to my family, my wife Lynne and two children Matthew and Rachel. Finally, without your marvellous support none of this would have been possible.

THANK YOU VERY MUCH.

FOLKS, THIS IS WHY HE'S DOUG CLEGG, THE LEGENDARY WHITING FISHERMAN, AND I'M NOT. A 1KG PLUS WHITING ON HIS FIRST CAST ON NATIONAL TELEVISION!! I WONDER HOW IT FELT AFTER BEING KISSED BY *TWO* FEROCIOUS LOOKING BEARDED BLOKES AND THROWN BACK.

The search for "big momma" whiting

EVERY KEEN WHITING FISHER WANTS TO CATCH A KING GEORGE WHITING OVER THE MAGIC KILO MARK. FOR MOST OF US FISHING IN THE EASTERN STATES, THIS IS ALMOST THE IMPOSSIBLE DREAM, BUT THE URGE IS STILL THERE. I HAVE A MATE IN WESTERN AUSTRALIA WHO IS A BIT OF A LEGEND ON WHITING AND HE IS ALWAYS TORMENTING ME WITH TALES OF ENORMOUS FISH. HIS NAME IS DOUG CLEGG AND I THOUGHT I MIGHT PUT THE ACID ON HIM AND SEE IF WE COULD COME UP WITH ONE OF THESE 'MYTHICAL' KING GEORGES ON NATIONAL TELEVISION. IT TURNED OUT THAT DOUGIE WASN'T KIDDING, THESE FISH ARE BIG MOMMAS!

It is a long way out west but when you finally make it to Rottnest Island, all the travelling is worthwhile. This beautiful little island is a real gem, with fantastic clear blue water on all sides. When the Dutch discovered it they mistook the quokkas for giant rats and so it was named 'Rats Nest' Island. Very romantic. I wonder if they lowered the rum ration after they left the island? We didn't have any rum on Cleggie's boat and the only giant things we wanted to see were giant whiting.

We anchored off the island on one of Doug's favourite clear sandy whiting spots and started to fish. The best area to find whiting in this part of the world is broken reef surrounding sand patches. The fish seem to feel comfortable schooling over the sand, but they have the security of a bit of reef to hide in if predators show up. The reef areas also provide plenty of tucker for these oversized fish.

It was obvious that we were in a good spot, but I expected to have to put in a monumental effort to pull a big momma into the boat. That's why the next part of the story is really hard to believe. I could honestly say I have never seen a live King George over a kilo in all my years of fishing around Victoria, and Doug Clegg pulled one up *first cast* on national television. Well, yibbida yibbida folks, he is Doug Clegg and I'm not!

This fish put up a great fight on Doug's light rod and he thought it might have been a flathead when it kept boring for the bottom. At the last minute we both recognised it as a whiting and I slid the net under it and hauled it into the boat. Fair dinkum, these whopper whiting are solid fish and they are worth waiting for. Just a beautiful fish–silver on the long streamlined belly–fawn on the back. I could imagine this one sizzling in the frying pan, but I just didn't have the heart to kill it. This fish is probably telling some strange stories, because it was kissed by two bearded ferocious-looking humans and then given its freedom. In Western Australia, it was only an average fish but anyone who saw the show from Victoria must have been drooling.

Big whiting in the west require different baits than those used in Victoria. The baits that Doug prepared looked more suited to white pointers than whiting–they were huge! The idea is to take a fresh octopus leg and strip off the suckers with a sharp knife. Then you cut the leg into strips about as long as your little finger. The next step is to rough-shell some coral prawns. To make the complete whiting bait, a coral prawn is threaded onto a wide-gape hook, and then a strip of tough octopus is added. The baits might have looked big to me, but the whiting thought that they were terrific and I guess that's what counts.

There is a bit of a trick to preparing a real Doug Clegg bait–you have to bash the occy around a bit with the handle of your knife so that it is nice and soft when a fish finds it. I keep telling the young punters out there to pay attention to detail–Doug is a successful fisherman because he attends to all the little things that make a difference at the end of the day.

We don't know exactly why the whiting are so big in this area, but Doug seems to think it is because the fish have not been commercially netted. Anglers pick off a certain amount of fish but the main population is basically untouched. There is some fisheries research going into this species and it looks as though the present bag limit is going to be reduced from thirty to twenty fish per person per day. As far as I am concerned twenty fish each, or forty between two mates, is enough to have some sport and a good feed at the end of the day, and that is what fishing should be all about. I take my hat off to Western Australian Fisheries for introducing these sensible regulations.

Both the Fisheries Department and Doug are doing a great job in Western Australia and it is good to see that some of the schools are now inviting Doug to give a series of lectures on fishing. This is a fantastic turn of events because it livens up the school day for the kids and it teaches them some valuable lessons. If you learn about fishing, you learn about biology, science and a lot of other subjects that have relevance in the school system.

Out at Rottnest we knocked off a few more whiting, and the old bearded burbler showed how much class it takes to catch wrasse on command! Fishing with Cleggie is a real experience, but on this occasion he really came up with the goods. One kilo whiting? No problem for Uncle Dougie.

FACT BOX

The search for 'big momma' whiting

ROD: Heavy butt, light tip. About 2.1m.
REEL: Light spinning. Egg beater style.
LINE: 4kg monofilament.
RIG: Paternoster–Hook 1\0 Long Shank.
DANGEROUS FEATURES: None.
TIME OF YEAR: All year round.
LOCATION: Rottnest Island, Western Australia.

FANGS FOR THE MEMORIES. GET A LOAD OF THE JACK LANG'S ON THAT
SPANISH MACKEREL. NO WONDER GREENIE'S GOT THEM ON HIS LIST OF
FISHING THINGS TO STEER CLEAR OF. WITH CHOPPERS LIKE THAT IT WAS
PROBABLY A CAN OPENER IN THE LAST LIFE. *(Paul B. Kidd)*

Bites, stings and spikes

DR DAVID GREEN IS A FIELD EDITOR WITH FISHING
WORLD MAGAZINE, AND HE ALSO RUNS AN EMERGENCY
SECTION OF THE GOLD COAST HOSPITAL ON THE
QUEENSLAND COAST. DAVID OFTEN RUNS INTO
PROBLEMS CAUSED BY OUR MARINE ANGLING SPECIES SO
HE IS WELL QUALIFIED TO SHOW US SOME DANGERS AND
HELP US STEER CLEAR OF THE 'NASTY' BITS ON OUR FISH.

Before David even started on his topic I found one deadly creature in south Queensland, and that was Peter Pakula's family cat, George. All George could see was a table full of delicacies and I really had my work cut out keeping him away from the specimens!

The first specimen that David picked to talk about was the deadliest one—the blue ringed octopus. Beware of any small octopus, because you just might be in danger if you pick one up and it bites you. The blue ring injects its toxin by biting with its small beak, and it is a killer. Small children are particularly at risk because this octopus is often found in tidal rock pools and shallows. It is also a cute-looking little animal that just asks to be picked up. The best way to avoid trouble with this little beastie is to warn your children not to pick up any small occy. As with most things in rock pools, it pays to look and not touch.

The next creature on the warning list was the red rock cod, also known as the flower pot. There are also several other related species around the country known as gurnards and scorpion fish that look similar and are equally dangerous. The problem with all these fish is their venomous spines. Each spike on the dorsal and some other fins has the potential to cause a nasty wound. The spikes are covered with a jelly-like substance that causes inflammation and pain. Some fish, such as Port Jackson sharks and elephant fish, take their defence one step further and they have actual venom sacs under the skin that feed toxin along the spines.

If you are stung by one of the rock cod species you will experience about four or five hours of excruciating pain. Any fish that is brightly coloured and has a large array of spikes should be treated with extreme caution.

If you do want to try and handle rock cod, about the only decent grip is afforded by putting your thumb in the mouth and gripping the lower jaw tightly. Your thumb will cop a bit of rasping, but you should be able to dodge the major spikes. I don't know about you folks, but the old bearded one is going for the nippers next time a flower pot comes on board–getting stung just doesn't seem worth it to me.

Next Greenie dragged out a fair-sized *Platycephalus fuscus.* Now don't run away and hide kids, because to you and me that just means a dusky flathead, one of the most common angling species in the country. Even though they are common, these fish cause David plenty of problems in his emergency department. The dusky has two very large, sharp and toxic spines on each side of his head, and when he is grabbed, he usually shakes his head rapidly. If you grab old *Platycephalus* by the middle, you are likely to have half a dozen rips in your hands in about one second. Apart from the pain of the toxin, the spikes of large flathead can do serious damage to the ligaments and joints of your fingers, so it pays to be cautious when you handle these fish.

So far all the dangerous fish we have looked at have been from saltwater, but one of our best-known freshwater sport fish, the Australian bass, has a bit of a secret weapon. David pointed out a well camouflaged, razor-sharp spine on the outside of the gill cover. Bass seem to be very popular fish at present and they are being stocked into many impoundments in our northern states, so a whole new generation of fishers will have a chance to catch one in the near future. It is important that these people are aware of the gill-spike because a carelessly handled bass can result in a finger being cut to the bone.

Now, from a fish that can cut a finger, to one that could take your whole arm off, and still want more! Spanish mackerel have a set of teeth that are just plain scary–don't let them near any part of your anatomy while they are alive. Even when they are dead, their teeth are so lethal that in Queensland they are not allowed to be marketed with their heads on. David Green reckons that more people have been seriously bitten by dead Spanish mackerel than live ones, so be wary, and chop the heads off your fish and throw them over the side as soon as possible! Even small mackerel should be treated with respect because they can still lop off a finger with ease.

If anything stings or bites you in the saltwater, it pays to put the affected part in hot water. Make the water as hot as you can stand, and keep the limb, or whatever, in it until some of the stinging sensation goes away. Seek medical advice if the injury is serious. It is great to have David Green on the Rex Hunt team because he is multi-talented and he knows how to get his message across. I hope between the two of us we might save you folks a bit of grief when something dangerous comes up.

FACT BOX
Bites, stings and spikes

THINGS TO WATCH OUT FOR: Teeth, spikes, small octopi.
REMEDIES: Hot water, medical assistance.

FISH, FISH, EVERYWHERE AND NOT A ROD IN SIGHT.
IT WAS HEART-BREAKING FOLKS! CHERRY PERRON HAND-FEEDS THE DIAMOND
SCALED MULLET AND MILK FISH AT *MAAAGNIFICENT* AQUASCENE ON DARWIN
HARBOUR. THANK GOD THEY'RE NOT PIRANHAS. *(courtesy Aquascene)*

Doctor's Gully fish frenzy

THIS WAS THE FIRST TIME IN MY LIFE THAT I HAD BEEN SURROUNDED BY FEEDING FISH WITHOUT HAVING A ROD IN MY HAND! AND IF I HAD SNUCK ONE IN, IT WOULD HAVE BEEN A CASE OF—YIBBIDA YIBBIDA—YOU'RE IN JAIL FOR THE NIGHT, REX! FEEDING THE FISH IN DARWIN HARBOUR HAS BECOME A WONDERFUL TOURIST ATTRACTION AND THEY TAKE A DIM VIEW OF ANGLER'S HOOKS IN THESE PARTS.

Aquascene is the brainchild of Marshall and Cherry Perron and it all started when they bought their harbour-side house at Doctor's Gully. The previous owner of the house had been feeding the diamond scaled mullet and the milkfish for about fifteen years, so the Perrons continued the tradition. Eventually word got around and more and more people wanted to participate in the ritual. The whole thing had the potential to get out of hand so it was decided that it would be run as a tourist attraction. Now Doctor's Gully is one of the most patronised tourist areas in Darwin.

After visiting it with my wife Lynne, I can see why. There are literally hundreds of fish chomping away on bread at every feeding session and the action is frantic! The diamond scaled mullet come right along the concrete feeding platform and take the bread from your outstretched hand. You can even give them a bit of a stroke as they go past without alarming them unduly. The sight of all these fish happily chewing away is enough to bring tears to an angler's eye.

9

The mullet create a bit of a disturbance but the real stars of the performance are the milk fish—the chanos chanos is a large streamlined fish that normally feeds on plankton, coral spawn and weed—they are not easily caught by anglers but when it does happen all hell breaks loose! To see hordes of these sickle-tailed bullets thrashing the water to froth in their efforts to wolf down a meal of bread is a memorable experience. Fishermen with a serious dose of fishing pox should probably stay away in case of heart attack!

Both Lynne and I enjoyed feeding the fish and it really does give you a feeling of being close to nature. The fish seem to know the feeding times off by heart and always turn up. Over the years the Perrons have learned to distinguish some of the regular visitors. Scungy the mullet earned his name because of his beaten-up appearance and he is easily recognised among the crowd. There have also been a number of big cod at times but they come and go.

Even non-anglers seem to have some affinity with fish, and the crowds visiting Doctor's Gully show no sign of diminishing. During the tourist season up to a thousand people a day come to watch the fish feeding and it is one of nature's wonders. If you are ever in the area make sure you call in for a look because you won't see anything quite like this anywhere else. Perhaps next time I visit, I could take just one small fishing rod—after seeing all the action this time, a spell in jail might be worth it!

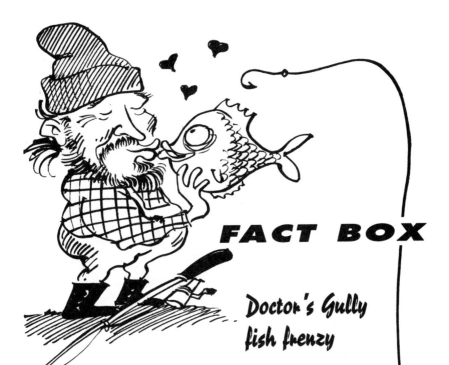

FACT BOX

Doctor's Gully fish frenzy

ROD: They wouldn't let me bring one.

REEL: Perhaps not.

LINE: Nope.

RIG: None.

BAIT: No way.

DANGEROUS FEATURES: Going to jail if you fish.

LOCATION: Doctor's Gully, Darwin Harbour.

THE MAN WITH THE MO, IN PERSON. THAT WOULD HAVE TO BE THE HAPPIEST
RAINBOW IN THE BUSINESS—BEING PHOTOGRAPHED WITH THE MOST FAMOUS
MO IN FISHING BEFORE BEING RELEASED. *(courtesy Bushy)*

Fly fishing
Eucumbene with Bushy

FLY FISHING HAS A REPUTATION FOR BEING ELITIST AND DIFFICULT, BUT FISHING IN THE BIG LAKE WITH BUSHY WAS A LOT OF FUN AND SIMPLE METHODS CAUGHT US FISH. FAIR DINKUM, THE ONLY TROUBLE THIS BLOKE HAS WHEN FISHING IS TRIPPING OVER THAT DIRTY BIG MOUSTACHE!

Lake Eucumbene is a fairly tough place to fish in the middle of summer–the grass is all burnt brown and the sun beats down mercilessly from a clear sky. In the evening though, a change takes place. The shadows soften and the temperature drops to a crisp cool level. We were fishing in the Frying Pan Arm of Lake Eucumbene, right up where the Frying Pan Creek runs into it, and the fish were starting to move.

Bushy ran us through some of the flies that work in Eucumbene and we looked at neoprene snail patterns, long green stick caddis flies and fat buoyant beetle patterns in case we had a calm evening and the Christmas beetles decided to fly and crash land into the lake.

During the previous week the fish had been coming up into the shallow water and eating the larva of the caddis moth. These little grubs hollow out a stick or a grass stalk and then live inside out of harm's way. Unless a hungry trout spots them that is! A lot of our viewers think that you need deep water to catch any species of fish, but that just isn't so. Trout especially love to fossick around in water that barely covers their backs, and that was what they were beginning to do as the afternoon shadows deepened.

This high country is something special. You feel as though you are on the roof of New South Wales, and there is a mile of room to move. The air is crystal clear and giant boulders stud the sides of the hills. Fishing takes us to some great locations and as the sun fades, Eucumbene works some sort of magic on the soul.

A rising fish brought me back to reality, and as others started to feed erratically along the bank, both Bushy and I were getting frustrated. The fish would rise in one spot, and a few seconds later they would be somewhere else. Fair dinkum, I thought, this game is worse than golf! I was sneaking along the bank trying to put my fly right in front of a dimpling trout, when there was a commotion in front of Bushy. He was standing precariously on a rock with his little Loomis fly rod bent in an ominous circle. Out in front, some large swirls showed that a fish was giving Bushy a run for his money, but eventually the steady pressure took its toll and a decent rainbow came into view. This was an average Eucumbene rainbow and it was just the sort of fish that brings people from all parts of the country to savour the Snowy Mountains fishing experience.

We slid the fish onto the grass and held it up for the camera. Eucumbene rainbows are really pretty fish and this female glowed with colour. Silver, lilac, red, and all covered in black spots–you wouldn't be dead for quids while you could chase fish like this! Bushy said that the fish only took his fly because he promised it I wouldn't kiss it. Well, that was a shame, because I'm Rex Hunt and he isn't, and the fish got a beautiful goodbye kiss from yours truly! There is nothing wrong with knocking them on the head for the frying pan either, but sometimes it doesn't seem to be the right thing to do, and it is a big thrill to watch a healthy fish swim free after it has given you a ton of fun.

Fly fishing is a great way to fish and I think that a lot more people are starting to give it a go. It isn't as complicated as it looks and the bloke with the black soup-strainer certainly looks as though he gets a kick out of it! It was just about dark as our rainbow swam out into the lake, so we gave the game away and headed home. There is a lot of camaraderie among fly fishers and it is great fun to fish with someone you get along with. Bushy and I had just enjoyed a good session and if there are folks out there that are thinking of giving the fly a go–get stuck into it, you will probably love it as much as I do.

FACT BOX

Fly fishing Eucumbene with Bushy

ROD: Loomis No 4 fly.

REEL: Golden Prince 5.

LINE: No 5 Teeny Floating.

RIG: Tapered leader, 4 pound tippet.

BAIT: Snail fly.

DANGEROUS FEATURES: None.

TIME OF YEAR: Summer.

LOCATION: Frying Pan Arm,
Lake Eucumbene,
New South Wales.

THIS IS WHAT ALL THE FUSS IS ABOUT FOLKS. IT'S A DOLPHIN *FISH,* NOT FLIPPER!
TO END THE CONFUSION, THEIR NAME HAS NOW BEEN CHANGED TO
MAHI-MAHI. AND I'LL TELL YOU WHAT, THEY'RE ALMOST AS GOOD TO EAT AS
THEY ARE TO CATCH. *(Paul B. Kidd)*

Dolphin fish delight in Western Australia

DON'T GET THE WRONG IDEA FOLKS, WE AREN'T ABOUT
TO BARBECUE FLIPPER! THESE DOLPHIN FISH ARE
BRIGHTLY COLOURED LEAPERS, BUT THEY ARE 100% FISH
AND IN NO WAY RELATED TO THE MAMMALS.
PHEW, NOW THAT WE HAVE GOT THAT STRAIGHT, I CAN
TELL YOU ABOUT THE GREAT DAY I HAD OUT WITH
NEIL PATRICK AS WE FISHED FOR THEM ALONG THE
CONTINENTAL SHELF OFF PERTH.

I could see this was going to be a high class trip from start to finish. Just to get to the boat, I had to walk through about ten million dollars worth of yachts. My old classmate from Mordialloc High, John Bertrand, would have been in his element here, even though I couldn't see any winged keels! The Perth Yacht Club is on the mighty Swan River and it was here I met up with Neil and boarded our swanky gameboat. Fair dinkum, there was a crew member to do just about every job on the boat and a few left over. Neil had certainly left nothing to chance on this trip to the shelf.

There is nothing quite like blasting along in a big fast game fishing boat with the prospect of a good day's fishing in front of you–there is something special about the salt spray and the grumble of the big diesel engines as the coast recedes rapidly. However, there are a couple of things that you have to think about at this stage. It is all very well to be hyped up and heading for the wild blue yonder, but where in the hell do you start to fish? On my fishing show, I keep trying to explain that everything we do in fishing has a reason. You have to plan every aspect of your fishing trips so they are successful, and on this occasion we were heading for a very definite location.

Neil Patrick was taking us to the edge of the continental shelf because that is where the northern currents strike the edge of a virtual underwater cliff. When the main current strikes this barrier, all sorts of violent upwellings and eddies result, and even on the surface a great mixing of nutrient-rich water occurs. This mixed-up water is a great environment for the plankton and small fish that predators such as dolphin fish feed on. Not only were we heading for the edge of the shelf, we were heading for a very special spot along that edge. Most of you would have fished from piers and jetties at some stage and you will have noticed that the best place to find fish is right next to the pylons. Fish love structure.

The Perth Game Fishing Club has placed a FAD in one of the best locations on the shelf to concentrate the pelagic fish, and that is exactly where we were headed. For newcomers to the world of game fishing, a FAD is not something like a pair of flared trousers! It is a Fish Attracting Device–hence the initials.

A FAD is anchored to the bottom with a long rope and it usually has some sort of underwater structure such as hanging strands of rope or nylon mesh to attract and hold fish in the immediate area. The whole thing does the same job as a jetty pylon–it concentrates the fish so you can target them. There is normally some form of structure above the water as well, to aid fishermen in pinpointing what is really a tiny target. With modern navigation aids such as the GPS system we were using, finding FADs is a lot easier than it used to be and we had no trouble in locating the one off Perth.

Things were looking good as we pulled up next to the FAD–birds were circling and fish were making occasional splashes around the structure. We dropped a couple of lures over the side and started to troll past the FAD, when whack! My rod-tip thumped over and a whirl of blue, yellow and silver flew out of the water and cartwheeled along the top. These fish are *maaagnificent,* they just go absolutely berserk when they are hooked and you haven't got a clue where they are going next.

The first fish took a Halco Trembler, which is not something you would buy at Fantasy Lane in Canberra but a 110g bibless minnow! These lures vibrate like crazy and are very noisy because they are packed with ball bearings. Tremblers are also as tough as nails and that makes them popular with charter skippers.

The dolphin fish were packed in hard under the FAD and that is fairly common behaviour for them. In fact, they often stack up under natural floating debris such as logs, pieces of timber, old buoys, and just about anything else that floats. Commercial fishermen in some countries set out trails of newspaper sheets in calm weather to attract fish. The sheets of paper float and the fish hide in the shade they provide. Neat trick!

The lures worked very well for us on the first few passes of the FAD, but the fish soon woke up to our tactics and stopped hitting. To counteract this, we pulled in close and started berleying with pilchard cubes. This really got the fish (and the mutton birds) excited, and with the aid of our underwater camera we could see them milling around and eating the pillies. Hooking the fish after that was child's play—it was just a matter of dropping down a cube on a simple running sinker rig and watching the fish gulp it down. We were using a 6kg main line with about a metre of 14kg monofilament for a trace. The trace was tied to a split ring that was attached to a double. A large bean sinker rode on the double and sat on the split ring. This sinker was only necessary to pull the bait down before the ravenous mutton birds got to it.

Watching a school of dolphin fish feeding underwater has to be one of the best experiences you can have. The light flashes off them as they dart around and they just illuminate the water under the boat incredibly. I guess the water out on the shelf helps to highlight the event as well, because it is absolutely clear.

This sort of fishing is the pay-off for a lot of long hard hours in my game, so the old bearded one did plenty of whooping and hollering while the dolphin tribe danced the light fantastic across the waves. I get a lot of fun out of bringing action like this to all the

My WA offshore fishing mate, Neil Patrick, with some of the fabulous Halco lures he makes at his Fremantle factory. Neil's lures are so good that you have to hide in the cabin to put one on the line for fear of the fish jumping into the boat to get at it. *(Paul B. Kidd)*

fishing people that, for one reason or another, can't make the trip out to the game fishing grounds and it makes the hard slog all worthwhile.

Dolphin fish are among the best table fish in the sea, so we kept a couple for lunch, but they are just so beautiful that it wasn't difficult to release the rest. It doesn't matter what we target in the fishing scene, we have to respect our fish and take only enough for our immediate needs. If I ever get one message across to our young anglers, it is this–don't be greedy. We certainly had a ball on the dolphin fish and we left plenty behind to make somebody else's day a happy one!

FACT BOX

Dolphin fish delight in Western Australia

ROD: 6kg game rod.
REEL: Shimano TLD 15 or 20.
LINE: 6kg.
RIG: Running sinker.
BAIT: Pilchards, lures.
DANGEROUS FEATURES: Being whacked with tail.
LOCATION: The continental shelf off Perth.

BREAM AND TREVALLY ARE A COMMON FISH AROUND THE PIERS AND JETTIES OF AUSTRALIA. *(Paul B. Kidd)*

Family fishing at Flinders Island

*PUT THE OLD BEARDED BURBLER ON ANY PIER WHERE
THERE IS A FISH OR TWO AND HE IS AS HAPPY AS A LARK.
I GUESS I LIKE PIER FISHING SO MUCH BECAUSE IT GOES
RIGHT TO THE HEART OF ANGLING. IT ISN'T COMPLICATED
AND YOU CAN CONCENTRATE 100% ON FISHING.
I TRAVEL ALL OVER THE WORLD CHASING FISH BUT I STILL
HAVEN'T LOST THAT COMMON TOUCH. I DON'T THINK IT
MATTERS IF YOU ARE A KID OR A MILLIONAIRE, YOU CAN
HAVE FUN ON A JETTY. ESPECIALLY IF THAT JETTY IS
SITUATED AT LADY BARRON ON THE SOUTHERN
EXTREMITY OF FLINDERS ISLAND.*

This is the sort of fishing that puts a bit of warmth back into the old Rex Hunt soul. I had my son Matthew with me, and Missy the dog also came along for the ride. The good news is that we stumbled onto a hot bite, and had silver trevally knocking us off all over the shop.

This particular jetty is in a magnificent spot. As you look out to sea, the rugged islands and the steep headlands disappear into the mist. Spectacular scenery and, as it turned out, spectacular fish. Silver trevally are great fish to catch off any pier. They fight like hell and when you hook them they head for the pylons every time. At Lady Barron the fish were pretty big too, and they really gave us a work-out on the light tackle that we were using. These fish have very soft mouths, so it is difficult to keep them from wrapping your line around the piles. The trick is to pull as hard as you dare, but to use a rod that has plenty of bend in it. The rod-god, Garry Marsh, made me up a couple of very light rods just for this type of fishing and they really do the job. Apart from the fight that they put up, silvers are an attractive angling proposition for another reason–they are great tucker!

Matthew and I were having a ball, and the size of the fish we were catching was around a pound and a half in the old measure. Great fun on the light gear, and good chewing. These fish didn't get the famous Rex Hunt kiss, they were due for an appointment with the frying pan later in the day!

I think the reason I love pier fishing so much is that you don't need an expensive boat, or a heap of expensive gear. It is a very easygoing type of angling that gives everyone a chance to fish.

Most of us spend too little time with our children, and I am no exception. On this trip I had a chance to talk with the young bloke and he seemed surprised that I still had plenty of enthusiasm for little fish off piers. I have never been one to pull my punches and I told him straight that I still had the common touch and that he should remember where he came from as well. 'Come to think of it,' I said. 'I never want you to forget where you came from either, mate. And that was in the back of my car at the Oakleigh drive-in in 1972!' And that was absolutely *maaagnificent!*

FACT BOX

Family fishing at Flinders Island

ROD: Light and whippy.

REEL: Egg beater style.

LINE: 2kg.

RIG: Paternoster.

BAIT: Squid.

DANGEROUS FEATURES: Spike under ventral fin of trevally.

LOCATION: Flinders Island.

THIS IS WHAT SHANE MENSFORTH PROMISED ME BUT COULDN'T PRODUCE—A
1KG PLUS WHITING. I RECKON THE REAL REASON THAT HE TOOK ME TO A
LOUSY SPOT WAS BECAUSE HE'S A CROWEATER AND THEY'VE NEVER FORGIVEN
US FOR WINNING THE GRAND PRIX OFF 'EM.

(Shane Mensforth)

The one kilo whiting that wasn't

SHANE MENSFORTH GUARANTEED ME A 1KG WHITING
OFF KANGAROO ISLAND, BUT IN THIS GAME IT DOESN'T
PAY TO COUNT YOUR FISH BEFORE THEY ARE IN THE
FRYING PAN! I HAD TO WHISPER WHAT WAS GOING TO
HAPPEN TO HIM IF HE DIDN'T PRODUCE THE GOODS,
BECAUSE YOU CAN'T SAY THAT SORT OF THING ON
NATIONAL TELEVISION! WE HAD PERFECT CONDITIONS,
THE RIGHT BAIT, AND THE BEST WHITING GUIDE AROUND.
WHAT WE DIDN'T HAVE BY THE END OF THE DAY WAS A
1KG WHITING. DEATH BY BUNDI BUNDI LOOKED A
DEFINITE POSSIBILITY FOR SHANE!

Fishing isn't just a matter of counting up all the kilos of dead fish that you can accumulate in a day. There is a lot more to it than that. I don't get to spend enough time with my fishing mates so when I do, I like to have a bit of fun. Shane and I take the mickey out of each other whenever we meet, and on this trip you had to be keen to get in first! Shane poked fun at my flimsy looking whiting gear, and he reckoned that his big South Australian fish would turn it inside out. 'In your dreams, Shane!' I countered by suggesting that he was just dirty because Victoria had picked up the Grand Prix!

After having our bit of fun, we packed the gear into Shane's boat and headed out to the supposed 1kg whiting spot. We absolutely blasted past the burnt brown hills and the rugged rocky outcrops in Shane's boat because there wasn't even a breath of wind. As we raced across the water, a pod of dolphins followed us and jumped in front of our bows in immaculate formation. It really does your heart good to see a group of 'Flippers' having fun with human sea-goers. The water looked fantastic when we finally arrived at our spot. It was so clear and blue it would just about make a born and bred Victorian cry.

Once we were settled we sorted out our tackle. The rig we eventually chose is very important for fishing in deep water. Old Bert Paternoster probably wouldn't have had a clue how much pleasure his rig would eventually give to Australian fishermen, but it is used for many different fish species every day in this country. We rigged the Paternoster by tying a 90g sinker to the bottom of the trace, and then tying two droppers above it. When using a threadline reel (better known as an egg beater) we lower the Paternoster rig to the bottom with just enough pressure so it doesn't tangle on the way down. The best way to do this is to release the drag on your reel until the weight of the sinker takes the rig down. This way, the rig makes it to the bottom intact and you have the best possible chance to catch a fish. If you just flip the bail-arm and let it rip, as you would when performing an ordinary cast, you risk the whole set-up tangling on the way down and lying in a real mess on the bottom.

Once our rigs were in productive territory, I asked Shane what type of bottom we were fishing on. Apparently there isn't much structure where we were fishing, just the occasional ledge. We were anchored up over a small drop-off but the action was slow, at least as far as 1kg whiting were concerned. Shane managed to pull up a double-header with a blue morwong on the bottom hook and a sergeant baker on the top. These morwong are a great looking fish with long feathery fins and blubbery mouths—and according to Shane they aren't bad tucker either. I wouldn't let the big fella from South Australia get away with anything though, good fish they might have been, but 1kg whiting, they weren't! It was up to me to at least catch the right species, and I will admit that the whiting I caught would have been a ripper back home. Sorry, Shane. We weren't back home, and the fish did not weigh 1kg.

By now the pressure was really on and I think that I had Shane on the run. Sure enough, the sun sank lower and lower and eventually we had to give the game away. I guess that the fish must have known I was coming, or Shane was really cranky about the Grand Prix and he took me to a barren spot on purpose! Oh well, there are probably worse things than death by bundi bundi!

FACT BOX

The one kilo whiting that wasn't

ROD: Whippy tip, solid butt.
REEL: Egg beater.
LINE: 4kg.
RIG: Paternoster.
BAIT: Pipi.
DANGEROUS FEATURES: None.
TIME OF YEAR: Summer.
LOCATION: Kangaroo Island, South Australia.

SUPERB ROCK HUT CREEK ON THE NSW HIGH PLAINS NEAR COOMA.
RIDING HORSES AND CATCHING TROUT IN SURROUNDINGS LIKE THIS IS
PRETTY HARD TO TAKE. *(Steve Starling)*

Wild Bill Hunt fishes Rock Hut

I THOUGHT IT WOULD BE A FAIR SWAP. SARAH SPENCER WAS GOING TO TEACH ME TO RIDE A HORSE. AND I WAS GOING TO TEACH HER HOW TO CATCH A TROUT IN THE FAMILY DAM AT ROCK HUT CREEK ON THE NEW SOUTH WALES HIGH PLAINS NEAR COOMA. AS IT TURNED OUT, I THINK I HAD THE EASIER JOB!

I guess that the horse thing went reasonably well, although the sight of a 110kg Rex Hunt galloping across the prairie isn't easily forgotten! Tootsie (my horse) will probably never be the same again after my impressive gallop, but I think that any adventure that doesn't end in a broken neck is an unqualified success. Teaching Sarah to catch a trout was definitely the easy part of the story.

The Spencer property is a great place to be, whether you are riding or fishing. Set at the end of a long winding gravel road in the middle of some magic high plain scenery, the property boasts two picturesque dams that are stocked with rainbow trout. Even though the dams are on the property, Sarah had never been keen enough to try her hand at fishing. That was just about to change.

I always get a kick from putting learners on the right track, so setting Sarah up with a nicely balanced outfit and showing her how to cast was no problem. She took to winding with her left hand straight away and that always makes the job easier. With any sport, it is better to start with the correct technique first up, and as far as fishing is concerned, that means winding with the left hand. With a normal threadline reel, hold the rod with your master hand and wind with the other. If you are a left hander, hold your rod with the left and wind with the right. It sounds a bit complicated, but isn't difficult to master.

Putting slimy, wriggly worms on the hook is a different matter, and Sarah was happy to leave that part of the job to me. Fair enough, she did put the bridle on my horse! We decided to fish with a float because that way Sarah would know exactly when the fish had taken the bait. There must be plenty of fish in the Rock Hut Creek dams because we didn't have to wait long for the little float to slide under the water and sneak some slack line off the reel. Sarah struck, and eventually between the two of us we slid a fat rainbow trout up on the grass. Fishing and kids go together like strawberries and cream—if you take the time to show them how it is done, they usually have a ball.

I asked Sarah what she wanted to do after she left school and it took a bit of persuasion before she would tell us that she wanted to be a ballet dancer. That is a great thing to aim for, and I want to say to all the kids out there that you can achieve anything you want. When I was a kid, I had no confidence at all, but now I am doing what I love to do. If any of you have an ambition, go for it. Sarah wants to be a ballet dancer, you might like to be a train driver. You might even want to sell pies at the footy and give one to the old bearded burbler when he is on 3AW. It doesn't matter what you are or who you are, if you can do what you want to do, that is what life is all about.

FACT BOX

Wild Bill Hunt fishes Rock Hut

RAINBOW TROUT

ROD: Light spinning.

REEL: Egg beater.

LINE: 2kg.

RIG: Float and split shot.

BAIT: Earthworms.

DANGEROUS FEATURES: None.

TIME OF YEAR: Autumn.

LOCATION: Monaro,
New South Wales.

PETER PAKULA WITH HIS *MAAAGNIFICENT* SNAPPER AND IT WASN'T EVEN TAKEN
ON ONE OF HIS INCREDIBLE LURES THAT HAVE MADE HIM A LEGEND ALL OVER
THE WORLD. BUT IT GOT HIM GRINNING LIKE A CARPET SNAKE THAT HAD JUST
CRAWLED OUT OF A CHICKEN HOUSE.

Southport snapper

YOU NEVER KNOW WHAT IS GOING TO GET IN ON THE ACT WHEN YOU DROP SOME BERLEY IN THE DRINK OFF SURFERS PARADISE. THIS TIME MY OLD MATE PETER PAKULA HIT THE JACKPOT WITH HIS BIGGEST EVER 'REDDIE' AND FOLLOWED UP WITH SOME RIPPER SPANISH MACKEREL.

Just getting to the fishing grounds can be a challenge in some locations and the Southport Bar has a dubious reputation. My companion for the day, Peter Pakula, is an old hand at bar crossings so I was able to sit back and relax. If you haven't tackled many bars, there are a few basic principles that you should be aware of. The first one is that if you have any doubts about the situation, don't go out! If you have had a good look at the conditions and you are confident, then tackle the pressure waves with a reasonable forward momentum. That doesn't mean full throttle! If you are too heavy-handed the boat will fly up in the air and land heavily stern first. If you dunk the bum of your boat in the surf hard, you are likely to drown your motor and then you are in all sorts of trouble.

Once you make it over the bar you have to think about getting back. This is usually easier than going out and the best method for returning is to put the bow of the boat just behind a big wave and keep on its shoulder all the way over the bar. If conditions have deteriorated while you have been fishing, don't hesitate to put your life jacket on. If you have kids on board it is a good idea to put a jacket on them anytime you are crossing a bar. Always notify the coastal patrol when you are going to sea and tell them when you intend to return. It takes experience to be really competent in crossing ocean bars and it pays to go easy while you are learning.

PAKULA AND THE SPANISH MACKEREL WITH CHOPPERS THAT COULD BITE
THROUGH A BROOM STICK. THE ONLY WAY THAT THE OLD BEARDED BURBLER
WAS GETTING NEAR THAT THING WAS WITH A DONGER. AND I'LL TELL YOU
SOMETHING ELSE, IT WASN'T REAL BAD FOR DINNER THAT NIGHT EITHER.

The best way to learn is by fishing with an old hand for a while.

We anchored off Surfers Paradise and there was a fair current howling south. Our berley was also heading in that direction and we needed a little bit of lead on our baits to make sure they stayed in the trail. Just about everywhere that we go, the old West Australian pilchard is a top bait and it is no different in Queensland. I rigged up a 3\0 chemically sharpened red hook, sewed it through a whole pillie, and dumped it into the trail. I put this rig out on my Shimano overhead outfit and then set my threadline with a similar bait tied to a wire trace. This one was for mackerel. They have evil teeth and will cut through normal monofilament as though it wasn't there. The Shimano Bait Runner is a great reel for this job because you can hit the free-spool lever and lower the bait easily down the trail.

I love it when a plan comes together—we had just watched our baits slide into the wide blue yonder when two fish hit us at once. This is what it is all about folks—fishing at its best! We were both winning our battles with these strong fish but unfortunately my hook pulled on the way up and the fish got a reprieve. Peter was luckier and his fish stayed on as he struggled to lift it to the surface. This is the stage of the fight where many big fish are lost. There is very little stretch left in a short length of line so if the angler makes a mistake and pulls too hard, that is the end of the ball game. Peter stayed cool and there was no mistaking the silver sides and the big hump on the head as the fish came nearer—this was an old man snapper! Peter Pakula has caught more big marlin than I have had hot dinners but this snapper had him grinning like a Cheshire cat. It turned out that this was Peter's biggest snapper so far and we were lucky enough to capture it on national television. These are magnificent fish and a close look at this one showed the flashing colours, the shining scales and the massive head—fantastic!

Things went quiet for a while after the big snapper but perseverance finally paid off for the big fella. My reel went absolutely berserk and as the line raced out I knew that we had run into old Manual Labour—the Spanish mackerel! I was well equipped with my trusty Shimano 30 two speed reel but these fish are incredibly fast and the line just kept disappearing off the spool. When your line goes sideways and creates a spurt of water about 30cm high as it travels, you know you have hooked a serious fish. Eventually my mackerel started to tire and I cranked it steadily back to the boat. We could see the fish in the clear water as it arced back and forth across our wake, and it looked to be about 120cm long.

I took it carefully and Peter made no mistake with the gaff. It takes skill to hit one of these fish in the head but that is the safest way to gaff them and it also keeps the fillets on both sides of the fish undamaged. Mackerel are one of the all time great eating fish and this one was destined for the Rex Hunt nose-bag! Landing big fish requires teamwork, and it is a good idea to have the skipper drive the boat ahead slowly as the fish is led to the back of the boat. This tactic makes it harder for the fish to wrap the line around the propeller. Peter took care of all the precautions and that is the reason that we came up trumps with the Spaniard.

Once the fish was on board Peter commented on the razor-sharp teeth. Fair dinkum, the teeth on a mackerel are just lethal–they can cut straight through a broomstick, so lopping off a finger or two would be child's play. The best thing to do when you put one in a boat is to introduce it to the 'donger' as soon as possible.

Peter Pakula is a top fisherman and he pulled a great day out of the old piscatorial hat for us at Southport. We could see the high rise buildings from where we were fishing but I would much rather be on the water than in a casino. Big snapper and prime mackerel–it doesn't come much better than that!

FACT BOX

Southport snapper

ROD: 15kg light game.

REEL: Shimano two speed game reel.

LINE: 15kg monofilament.

RIG: 3\0 hook, light sinker.

BAIT: West Australian pilchards.

DANGEROUS FEATURES: Teeth on mackerel.

TIME OF YEAR: Autumn.

LOCATION: Southport, Queensland.

THE ONLY THING WRONG WITH MAGGOTS AS BAIT IS THAT THE OLDER YOU GET, THE HARDER IT IS TO THREAD THEM ON THE HOOK. BUT IT'S WORTH THE EFFORT BECAUSE THEY'RE ABOUT THE BEST BAIT AROUND. *(Ted Rose)*

Maggot mania

I GET PLENTY OF STICK FROM MY MATES—SOME OF THEM RECKON I'VE GOT A CUSHY JOB TRAVELLING AROUND AUSTRALIA TO BRING YOU FOLKS INTERESTING FISHING STORIES. TODAY I GOT TO LOOK AT AN ASPECT OF FISHING THAT REALLY STINKS, AND NOBODY VOLUNTEERED TO HELP ME! YOU GUESSED IT FOLKS, THIS IS ALL ABOUT ONE OF THE BEST BAITS AROUND—MAGGOTS! TERRY SHEPHARD IS THE COARSE FISHING GURU AND HE GIVES US THE LOWDOWN (AND I MEAN THAT SINCERELY) ON BREEDING THESE MAGNIFICENT CREATURES!

I met Terry on the banks of my beloved Goulburn River to see just what can be caught on the dreaded maggot. Terry had arrived earlier and his keeper net was alive with small, spotted brown trout. It goes to show that around the Thornton area the old Goulburn is still healthy. I would have liked to throw a line in myself, but had to get down to business and check out this maggot breeding caper.

Terry soon put me straight on how to get started. The first step is to acquire some lambs' hearts and put them in a box. Leave the lid off and every fly in the area will find them and start to lay little crawling type things on them. Yuck! Leave the hearts exposed for a couple of hours so the flies have a good shot at them. If you leave the meat exposed for too long, too many maggots will be produced and they will be stunted and small. Big healthy maggots are best so it pays to cover the meat after two hours.

The next step is to cover the whole mess with fine, dry saw-dust. Some people use pollard or bran but if the weather is warm, maggots tend to generate a lot of heat and then they sweat. If this

A LOT OF FOLKS SAY THAT COARSE FISHING GURU TERRY SHEPHARD AND I COULD BE TWINS, BUT I JUST CAN'T FIGURE OUT WHY. COULD IT BE THE BEARD? OR MAYBE IT'S THAT MAGNIFICENT CROP OF HAIR, JUST LIKE MINE.

happens the whole thing degenerates into a sticky, gluey mess!

Terry had a box of meat that had been exposed to flies a couple of days previously and he showed me how to shake the big maggots off what was left of the meat. If you have a weak stomach, stop reading here, because I am about to tell you that this particular part of the scheme is diabolical and there is no way around the fact that everything stank to high heaven. Mate, if you think your job stinks, you are joking! Terry claimed that a little vanilla essence might have helped. That is like saying that a little money might balance the South American national debt!

After the gents have been shaken from the meat, they are put through a sieve to separate them from the sawdust. Once this process has been completed the maggots can be laid in fresh sawdust and the worst is over. If the gents are kept at room temperature they will rapidly turn into casters (the chrysalis form) and then into adult flies. To prevent this happening you can keep them in containers in the fridge where they will last indefinitely. If you put them in plastic butter containers, make sure you are concentrating when you get up for that late night snack. I think gents spread all right, but I am not too sure about the taste!

If you are organised I can see that breeding your own maggots isn't all that difficult, even if it is all that smelly! Successful fishing is about 90 per cent preparation, so if you put a bit of work into preparing a deadly bait such as maggots, you should catch more fish. I won't say that it was a pleasure fishing with my mate Terry on the Goulburn (pheeew!), but I certainly did learn a few tricks of the maggot trade.

TRY AS HARD AS HE COULD, ALL ROD McDAFFREY COULD FIND ME THIS DAY
WAS A YELLOW–TAILED GRUNTER ALSO KNOWN LOCALLY AS AN ESTUARY PERCH.
(Brian Hutchinson)

Way down on the "Swannee" River

*I GUESS WE HAD BETTER MAKE THAT THE SWAN RIVER
BEFORE ANYONE GETS THE WRONG IDEA FOLKS. FAIR
DINKUM, I FLEW ABOUT NINE MILLION MILES TO GET
THERE, AND EIGHT MILLION OF THEM WERE OVER DESERT.
WHEN YOU FLY IN, PERTH LOOKS LIKE A BEAUTIFUL OASIS
AND THE SWAN RIVER IS MAJESTIC AS IT WENDS ITS WAY
SLOWLY THROUGH THE RIVER GUMS. I WAS THERE TO FISH
WITH ROD MCDAFFREY BECAUSE HE CUT HIS TEETH
ALONG THIS WATERWAY AND JUST ABOUT KNOWS THE FISH
BY NAME.*

Rod is a local character and loves his fishing. He isn't a tackle shop operator or a professional guide; he is just a typical keen fisherman who loves his hobby. I get a real kick from travelling around Australia and fishing with new people in different locations. Rod had brought me to a section of the river about 40km upstream from Perth and it would be hard to imagine a more idyllic spot. The water is clear, the grass is lush and the shady trees hang over the bank to keep the sun off poor old fishermen like me.

We finally selected a spot that looked good and set our gear up on the bank. Now, McDaffrey sounds a bit like Gaddafi and one of Rod's buckets was making a suspicious humming noise—was the bearded burbler going to end up fried to a crisp on the banks of the Swan? No folks, it wasn't a bomb, it was an aerator to keep one of the best baits in the business alive and kicking.

Live prawns are deadly just about anywhere you use them and

our man on the Swan had laid in a good supply. Good planning is the key to good fishing and I could see one of the reasons why Rod is so successful. The little aerator was humming away happily and churning out a supply of air that bubbled up through a special type of stone to give the live prawns a good supply of oxygen. This gadget makes all the difference when you are trying to keep any form of bait alive and the few bucks that it costs to buy one are well worth shelling out.

Even with the live bait things were quiet. Actually they were deathly quiet. Sometimes you have to break the rules a bit in fishing so I peeled the shell from one of the prawns and put the soft white meat on to the hook. I cast it out into the slow current and as it settled and the line tightened, something looked strange. Yep, the line was going against the flow of the stream–I lifted my long rod and felt the strong throbbing pull of an active fish. This was more like it!

It wasn't a monster, but what a fat, healthy specimen of a bream it was. This was a tough little male in absolutely top form and ready to spawn. I didn't want to interrupt his life too much, even though he was of a legal size, so I gave him the famous kiss and gently returned him to his natural element. He swam around a bit to get his bearings and then darted out to deeper water. That is the good thing about fishing, it doesn't have to be absolutely spectacular all the time–I really enjoyed knocking that little fella off, and releasing him back into a healthy environment made me feel great.

I love to muck around along the edges of our rivers and streams just as much now as I did when I was a kid back at Ricketts Point on the shores of Port Phillip Bay, and the thing that I want to emphasise is that fish are in any location for a reason. It isn't hard to see why they visit this section of the Swan. I pulled up a couple of the rocks lining the shore and there were plenty of big spider crabs clinging to them. Bream eat spider crabs just like the big fella knocks off Christmas dinner so this would be a prime fishing spot on its day. The Perth council have put in rubble along the river banks to minimise the erosion damage caused by the wakes of passing boats. This rubble has protected the bank, but it has also had another positive effect by promoting habitat that has been colonised by crabs, small fish and shrimps. This is a perfect example of progress working in with nature for the common good.

While I was playing kids in the water, Rod got a bit excited as the tip of his rod came to life and started to quiver. He gave the rod a jerk and hooked up. This fish gave up the ghost fairly quickly and Rod dragged it in. This was an interesting fish that I had not seen before. It was a yellow-tailed grunter, known locally as an estuary perch. These are a very pretty fish–the main body is bright silver with small black dots covering the whole surface. There are three or four dark blotches along the back and the tail is bright yellow with black tips. Apparently these fellows are a bit bony but quite edible. Rod explained that there is no size or bag limit on the species and they are regarded as a 'bread and butter' fish in the west. Further north they are regarded as good live bait for barramundi.

I think that the Channel 7 cameras scared off the majority of the fish that we were intending to catch, but I guess we can't always have a bonanza. As long as we have healthy river systems such as the Swan and good basic fishermen like Rod to fish in them, Australia will stay a great place to live.

FACT BOX
Way down on the 'Swannee' River

ROD: Long and whippy.
REEL: Shimano Threadline.
LINE: 3kg.
RIG: Running sinker.
BAIT: Live prawns.
DANGEROUS FEATURES: Fin spikes on bream.
TIME OF YEAR: Winter.
LOCATION: Swan River, Perth.

THE OLD BURBLER AND MY LONG-HAIRED MATE, TERRY SHEPHARD, JUST
DOING IT EASY ON THE MIGHTY GOULBURN RIVER. THAT LONG THING IN THE
WATER THAT COULD EASILY DOUBLE AS THE SYDNEY HARBOUR TUNNEL IS
TERRY'S 'KEEPER' NET.

Goulburn gobblers

THE LITTLE TROUT OF THE GOULBURN RIVER TURN
INTO GOBBLERS WHEN THEY SEE A WELL-PRESENTED
MAGGOT. YES, FOLKS, WE DECIDED TO LET TERRY
SHEPHARD BACK ON THE SHOW AFTER THE DREADED
MAGGOT DEBACLE EARLIER. THERE HAVE BEEN PLENTY
OF HOUSEWIVES HUNTING WHAT IS LEFT OF THE OLD
REX HUNT SCALP BECAUSE FISHERMEN HAVE BEEN
HIDING THEIR GENTS IN THE FRIDGE, BUT WE DECIDED TO
RISK IT AND LET TERRY SHOW US SOME OF THE FINER
POINTS OF COARSE FISHING.

I met Terry for our coarse fishing session at a spot on the Goulburn about two hours from Melbourne and you wouldn't believe the rig that he arranged on the end of my line. First he threaded on a funny looking thing like a bird cage gone wrong, and then he tied on a hook that was so small you couldn't see it! The cage holds berley and the smell gradually seeps out and attracts fish to the bait on the invisible hook. At least that is the theory! Fair dinkum, the experience of threading maggots on a midget hook, by the 'fat' end, makes me glad that I didn't take up brain surgery. You've got to be kidding! Terry wasn't kidding, and if you don't hook the maggots through the fat end, they die. I did as I was told and stuffed about four gents on the hook before throwing the whole thing out into the river. After that, it was back to the waiting game.

Well, we didn't have to wait long. The system certainly does work and Terry soon had a ripper little fish kicking on the bank. These Goulburn brownies are beautifully marked and as fat as butter. This one had no fin clipping in evidence so I guess it had been naturally spawned. Once he had dehooked the fish Terry carried it over to the keeper net. Fair dinkum, this net would have gone right across Albert Park Lake! You would need a fair-sized trawler to pull it if you decided to go into the prawn business–what I am trying to say is that this net was seriously big! Our maggot hurler reckoned that the fish recovered better if they had a chance to get themselves together in the net before they were turned back into the wild. Another plus for keeping them out of mischief for a while is the theory that freshly released fish have a way of telling their friends that all is not well in the area. Terry prefers to release all his fish at the end of the day.

I have always been an advocate for long rods but the ones these blokes use for coarse fishing could poke holes in the sky. When you think about it though, the long rods do a great job when you are coarse fishing. Everything in this game is fine–the hooks are tiny, the lines are like spider web and the baits are small. Long flexi rods cast the soft baits delicately, they don't strain the tiny hooks and they act as absolutely brilliant shock absorbers for the light lines. These rods are also great casting tools and they are capable of long casts to put the baits in front of fish. I was really getting the hang of this coarse fishing by the end of the session, and I could see that it is a very effective way to fish. I am a bit worried that Terry might be slowing himself down a bit though. I reckon he might be spending too much time at the hairdressers! He obviously doesn't recognise the value of my modern minimum-maintenance hairstyle! Mate, now that you are using the new fancy fishing gear, you will have to get with the strength and go for the high-tech haircut of the nineties!

FACT BOX

Goulburn gobblers

BROWN AND RAINBOW TROUT

ROD: Long, light specialist coarse fishing rod.

REEL: Small egg beater.

LINE: 1.2kg.

RIG: Baitfeeder, No 18 hook.

BAIT: Maggots.

TIME OF YEAR: Autumn.

LOCATION: Goulburn River.

JIM LUDDINGTON ON THE BOW OF HIS CHARTER BOAT *STRAIT LADY* HEADING
BACK INTO FLINDERS ISLAND, WHICH I HAVE SINCE RE-NAMED
GURNARD ISLAND. YOU'LL FIND OUT WHY IN THE STORY. *(Richard Eastwood)*

Gurnard Island

TECHNICALLY, WE WERE ON FLINDERS ISLAND, BUT
WHOEVER NAMED IT MISSED AN EVEN BETTER NAME.
THIS JUST HAS TO BE THE GURNARD CAPITAL OF THE
WORLD. JIM LUDDINGTON KNOWS MORE ABOUT THE
FISHING AROUND THIS ISLAND THAN ANYONE ELSE BUT ON
THIS TRIP EVEN HE COULD NOT SEPARATE US FROM
THESE EVIL, SPINY LITTLE MONGRELS.

Flinders Island is a fairly spectacular location. Stuck in the wilds of Bass Strait, its rugged countenance is hammered by ferocious winds and storms. Anything that is left standing just has to be tough. The hills and rocks are covered in straggly scrub and mist often hangs over the highest peaks. The very isolation and gauntness of the place is an attraction and if you want fresh air, it doesn't come any fresher than here.

Jim had taken us out on his charter boat *Strait Lady* and we were trying for flathead. I will repeat that we were trying for flathead but gurnard were making life unbearable. We dropped our baits over in the shallow water–we caught gurnard. We dropped our baits over the side in deep water–we caught gurnard. If we had dropped our baits in the bottom of the boat I reckon that we could have caught gurnard! Jim tried every trick in the book to avoid them, but you know the story by now–we caught gurnard! Normally Flinders Island has a very good flathead fishery but someone must have told the gurnard that we were coming and I can tell you that they are not camera shy; in fact they did their utmost to dominate the show. Just for the record, we did catch some flathead but on this particular trip the old you-know-whats had the game sewn up.

These and other very similar species of fish are caught in many places around Australia so it might pay to just offer a word of warning here. I don't want some poor kid to be dragged off to hospital after doing a Rex Hunt and kissing a gurnard! These things are piscatorial dynamite–if one stings you with one of its spikes you are in for a few hours of pain. Do not under any circumstances handle these fish carelessly. The best thing is to cut the line or get the hook out with a dehooker or a pair of long pliers. These critters are actually not too bad to eat and Jim showed us an interesting way to deal with them.

Carefully handling the fish by the head, Jim slices all the dorsal spikes right off the carcase of the fish. Next he cuts the spikes off the underside. Once this is done, the head is cut off and then the rest of the fish is skinned. This method gets rid of the dangerous spikes in a hurry and the end product is easily handled and quite tasty.

If you do get stung, a pressure bandage applied to the area will localise the pain and make it slightly easier to bear. Hot water will also help to control the pain. Needless to say we had plenty of scope for Jim's fancy method of handling gurnard on this trip!

As a last resort we headed for Chappell Island because Jim told us that the you-know-whats were not as thick there. I innocently enquired what it was like on the island and Jim told me that it was a terrific place to visit because it had a population of the biggest tiger snakes in the world. If you don't mind umpire!!! If there is one thing that I really can do without, it is 1.8m long tiger snakes!

And as if the snakes weren't bad enough, I think that Jim had told me a bit of a porky–the first fish that I pulled up from the waters of Chappell Island was the biggest bloody gurnard I have ever seen in my life! Oh well, life wasn't meant to be easy, and visiting Flinders Island with Jim Luddington is always a great experience.

FACT BOX

Gurnard Island

ROD: 1.8m, whippy tip, strong butt.

REEL: Light overhead or heavy egg beater.

LINE: 10kg monofilament.

BAIT: Squid strips or pieces of flathead.

DANGEROUS FEATURES: Toxic spikes on gurnard.

TIME OF YEAR: Summer.

LOCATION: Flinders Island.

THAT MAN WITH THE MO AGAIN. BUSHY WITH A BEAUT RAINBOW
THAT FELL FOR THE TROUT'S FAVOURITE TUCKER—A PLUMP MUDEYE.
YIBBIDA YIBBIDA, THEY JUST LOVE 'EM FOLKS. *(courtesy Bushy)*

Mudeye magic

*TROUT AND MUDEYES GO TOGETHER LIKE STRAWBERRIES
AND CREAM. THERE IS NO BIG MYSTERY IN CATCHING
TROUT ON THESE LITTLE CREEPY CRAWLIES—IT IS JUST A
MATTER OF GOING RIGHT BACK TO BASICS.
GET THE RIGHT BAIT. KEEP IT ALIVE. MAKE SURE YOUR
TACKLE IS RIGGED CORRECTLY, AND MAKE SURE THAT
YOU ARE FISHING IN THE RIGHT SPOT. KEEP IT BASIC AND
YOU CAN'T GO WRONG.*

Well, we did have the right bait and we were fishing in the Frying Pan Arm of Lake Eucumbene in the Snowy Mountains of New South Wales. The water was rising and trout were making rings as they sucked things gently from the surface. Everything looked about right for us to catch a fish.

Setting up a functional mudeye rig is fairly easy. I was using a plastic bubble float with an internal hollow stem. You can run the line through the float so that when a fish takes the bait he can pull the line through without feeling any drag. You can also fill any bubble float with water to add casting weight to your rig, and because the old H_2O is heavy stuff, it is possible to cast a mudeye rig a long way.

Once you have threaded the line through the float, you need to add some sort of stopper. The tried and true method is to cut a small cube of cork and then to put a slit in it with a razor blade. After you run the line through the float, just wrap it into the cut in the cork about three times. The float will slide down your line and then stop at the piece of cork. Leave about 25cm of line hanging from the cork and tie a small black swivel (No 14) to the end of it. After that it is a simple matter of tying on another short length of fine trace and finally attaching a small No 14 kendal kirby mud-eye hook. The little swivel is a vital addition to the rig because it takes out any line twist that occurs when you wind in the rig to check your bait. The cork cube will usually crumble up when a fish is hooked so it pays to cut a few before you start to fish.

Always grease your line with vaseline or mucilin to make it float along the surface—this prevents any drag when a fish eats the mudeye and swims away. If you don't use the grease, the line between you and the float will sink and a fish will nearly always feel the drag, drop the bait, and yibbida yibbida, that will be all folks!

I guess most people know what a mudeye is, but just in case you have been hiding in the piscatorial wilderness I had better explain that it is the larvae of the dragon fly. There are two common types of mudeyes around—one is the couta, which is the big long aggressive one, and the other is the spider, which is the small fat one commonly found in Lake Eucumbene. Both are great trout bait. On this expedition I was using spider mudeyes because they are a major food source for trout in the big Snowy lakes. Right where we were fishing I could see the cases of the mudeyes clinging on to the rocks along the water's edge. When mudeyes hatch into adult dragon flies, they swim to the edge of the water and crawl out onto rocks or thistle stems, then they split their shells, dry their wings, and fly away.

Now listen up kids and the old bearded burbler will let you in on the final secret when you are casting out your mudeye rig. Just before the whole shebang hits the drink, feather the outgoing line by putting your finger on the spool of your reel. This will slow the flight of the rig down and the mudeye and hook will hit the water first. If you don't take this precaution, the whole rig can land in a tangled mess and you won't catch a fish.

We had picked a real cracker of a morning (even if we did have to get up at 4am to do it!) to fish our mudeyes, and in the calm conditions I felt very confident as I picked up my long rod and pelted the rig out into the arm. I opened the bail arm and put the rod in the holder. It didn't take too long and sure enough my line started to sneak out of the guides. If everything is set up properly there is no hurry and it pays to let the fish get the bait well down. This time everything went right and when I lifted the rod I felt the plunge of a healthy fish. We had a bit of a tussle for a while but I soon realised that the fish was caught around an underwater obstacle. This was a bit hard to take because we really needed that fish for the cameras, but there is no point in panicking at any time when you are fishing so I just took my time and gradually worked away at the obstruction. Eventually something gave way and I pulled in a fat rainbow trout of around a kilo. This was a beautifully marked fish that really made my day. Fair dinkum, I must have the best job in Australia! This fish just looked so good that I couldn't put her in the old frying pan, so she ended up with the kiss of life and went back.

The sun was shining and the water was gin clear in the high Snowy Mountains–the fish were keen to knock off my mudeyes and I had my bum on a comfortable rock. To coin a phrase–it doesn't get any better than this!

FACT BOX

Mudeye magic

RAINBOW TROUT
ROD: Long whippy Gary Marsh special.
REEL: Small Shimano egg beater.
LINE: 2kg.
BAIT: Mudeye.
DANGEROUS FEATURES: None.
TIME OF YEAR: Summer.
LOCATION: Frying Pan Arm, Lake Eucumbene,
New South Wales.

AUSTRALIA'S PREMIER KNOT AND FISH ILLUSTRATOR AND 'REX HUNT'S
FISHING ADVENTURES' REGULAR, GEOFF WILSON, HOLDS ALOFT A COUPLE OF
TAMBOON BEAUTIES TAKEN ON THE DEADLY BERT PATERNOSTER RIG.
(courtesy Geoff Wilson)

Tamboon salmon

THE AUSTRALIAN SALMON HAS BEEN ONE OF THE MOST
USED AND ABUSED SPECIES OF FISH IN THIS COUNTRY.
HOUNDED BY SPOTTER-PLANES AND RUTHLESSLY PURSE
SEINED ALMOST TO EXTINCTION, THESE FISH ARE NOW
MAKING SOMETHING OF A MODEST COME-BACK.
THIS IS GREAT NEWS FOR A COUPLE OF REASONS.
WHEN CAUGHT BY AMATEURS THEY GENERATE A HUGE
AMOUNT OF MONEY AND WHEN TAKEN BY ROD AND LINE
THEY ARE QUITE A GOOD FOOD FISH. IT MAKES NO
SENSE TO ME TO WIPE OUT THIS GREAT FISH SO THAT THE
DEAD BODIES CAN BE SOLD FOR A PITTANCE AND USED
AS CRAYFISH BAIT OR CAT FOOD.
TAMBOON IS A REMOTE LOCATION ON THE VICTORIAN
NINETY MILE BEACH AND IT USED TO BE A MECCA
FOR SURF FISHERMEN.

When I first walked down to the beach I could see at a glance that conditions were not ideal. There was an offshore wind and the surf was very quiet. Salmon are fast and aggressive hunters and they love to feed right in amongst the crashing waves of a booming surf. It looked as though things were going to get very tough for the big fella on this trip, but when the going gets tough, the tough get cunning! It is no good going on a fishing trip and spitting the dummy if things aren't perfect. We didn't have a booming surf and we didn't have many waves at all, but at times like these you just have to do the best you can and try to put the odds back in your favour. I am a great believer in the power of berley so I mixed up an evil smelling brew and kept on throwing handfuls into the surf.

I knew the fish were around, because my son was out behind the break in my 5.5m Caribbean boat and he was pulling them in left, right and centre. Another mate of mine, Ian Clarke, had even launched his tinny and was also in on the action. But folks, the old bearded burbler was stuck on the beach and short of straining the back or bursting the 'poo poo' valve, he just couldn't make the distance! It is awfully frustrating when you fall about a 'poofteenth' short of the action.

Even though my friends were doing well, I should throw in a word of warning here, because fishing around the surf in boats is a very hazardous proposition most of the time. In a vigorous surf, air and water mix, and there are so many air bubbles trapped under the surface that the propeller of an outboard motor just can't get a grip. You only have to be stuck for a moment to be rolled by a bigger than average wave and then it can be, yibbida yibbida, that's the end of the road folks! On this occasion though, everything was just so flat that the blokes in the boats were safe, and they were cleaning up.

Meanwhile, back on the beach, I had no option but to keep on throwing berley and hoping that I could bring the fish within casting range. There were a few birds working in closer, which was a good sign, and then I nailed a little salmon. Things were looking up. These fish are terrific battlers, even at the juvenile stage. This one still had the bars and spots that all young salmon show. As they mature the back turns grey and the sides are silver without many spots. Small salmon are great on the barby or in a bit of egg and breadcrumb, but I took mercy on this one, gave him the kiss, and watched him scoot through the shallows and back into the surf. This was more like it!

I threw a bit more berley and rebaited the old Bert Paternoster rig. In light conditions such as these it pays to keep your rig delicate. I was using two 1\0 hooks tied on long droppers and a small sinker that allowed me just enough weight to cast into the break. The next bite was a quick rat-tat-tat, and sure enough a little flattie had knocked off the pipi. How these little fish manage to swallow baits that are bigger than their heads amazes me. This wasn't what I was after but it did show me that the berley was slowly but surely

'**R**ex Hunt's Fishing Adventures' tackle maestro, Jim Allen, loves catching Tassie trout on fly when he's not running his chain of Compleat Angler stores.

Shimano boss, John Dunphy, has been with the Rex Hunt TV show from the beginning. Steve Starling and I caught up with him at the annual Fishing Tackle Show. (*Paul B. Kidd*)

𝓕abulous Freddy Jobson, a 'Rex Hunt's Fishing Adventures' regular, releasing a Murray cod. *(Steve Starling)*

*S*ometimes it gets a little crowded while filming...like this day on Sydney Harbour. *(Paul B. Kidd)*

*S*igning autographs at Sydney's HMAS Platypus during filming segments for the show. *(Paul B. Kidd)*

*S*unset at Flinders Island, my favourite Bass Strait fishing spot. *(Steve Starling)*

*I*t doesn't get much better than this folks. Presenting flies to big Eucumbene rainbows. *Maaagnificent. (Steve Starling)*

*T*hese days kids can choose fishing on their sports day. What a sensible idea. *(Paul B. Kidd)*

*F*abulous Flinders. One of my favourite places in the Bass Strait with rock, beach, estuary, offshore and pier fishing. A fabulous place for a family fishing holiday. *(Steve Starling)*

*T*he 'Rex Hunt's Fishing Adventures' film crew (l to r); the old Bearded Burbler, director Bob Grieve, cameraman John Hawley, executive producer/manager Greg Numa and sound assistant Tony (Jacky-Jacky) Dickinson. *(Paul B. Kidd)*

_W_ith a Sydney caught trevally—one of the toughest fighters of them all.
(Steve Starling)

doing its job and attracting fish.

Finally the old rod tip really thumped hard, and a reasonable salmon cartwheeled out of the shore-break. He put up a great fight and this allowed me to run through the surf landing technique for newcomers to surf fishing. The main thing here is not to rush the operation. There is a temptation to keep on winding the fish in as the wave rushes back down the beach. If you do keep on winding, the increased pressure often pulls the hook or breaks the line. The best thing to do when the water recedes is to just hold the rod and steady the fish against the backwash. When the wave returns, walk up the beach steadily until the fish is aground and then you can pick it up. This time everything went according to plan and a 1kg Australian salmon made it up the beach.

Fresh salmon are good to eat if you handle them the right way as soon as you catch them. The trick is to put them out of their misery in a hurry by breaking their necks. This also starts the bleeding process that improves the flavour. The fish should be buried head-first in the sand so that they stay cool and all the blood can run out of them. In my mind's eye I could see this fish sizzling on the old Rex Hunt barbecue, so he got the treatment rather than the kiss! Stoke up the fire and cool the tinnies because we eat in style tonight!

FACT BOX

Tamboon salmon

ROD: 3.6m surf rod.
REEL: ABU overhead.
LINE: 10kg.
RIG: Paternoster, 1\0 hooks, light sinker.
BAIT: Pipi.
DANGEROUS FEATURES: None.
TIME OF YEAR: Summer.
LOCATION: Tamboon Inlet, Ninety Mile Beach, Victoria.

Bleak, miserable, overcast, dull and bloody freezing. Just another
day on Lake Sorell. But Foxy (left) knows better than to worry
about trivial matters like being frozen to death. Just get out the
wet flies, take it like a man, and you'll wind up with a bag of beauties
like this—fresh, wild trout for dinner.

Foxy and the freezing trout

WELL, I HAD BEEN SUNBURNT IN QUEENSLAND, BLOWN
TO BITS IN WESTERN AUSTRALIA, AND THEN I WAS
ALMOST FROZEN TO DEATH IN TASMANIA IN THE MIDDLE
OF SUMMER. FAIR DINKUM, WOULD YOU GIVE A POOR OLD
FISHERMAN A BREAK! JOHN FOX KNOWS ALL ABOUT
TROUT IN THE APPLE ISLE AND HE GOT ME OUT IN THE
MIDDLE OF LAKE SORELL IN 90CM HIGH WAVES WITH A
FLY ROD. I RECKONED I WAS FIGHTING A LOSING BATTLE,
BUT I ALWAYS SAID THAT YOU HAVE TO PERSEVERE
WHEN THINGS ARE TOUGH, AND THIS LAKE WAS FULL OF
TROUT, SO I GUESS I JUST HAD TO TRY TO KEEP UP
WITH MY MAN IN TASSIE.

You just couldn't believe the day that we copped for our fly fishing session in Lake Sorell. It was blowing a gale, the surrounding hills were shrouded in mist, and it was bloody freezing! The worst part about it was that Foxy thought that the conditions were great for a bit of wet-fly fishing! Sure Foxy. As if things weren't bad enough, my intrepid guide wanted me to wade out into the middle of the lake so that I could fish on top of a shallow weedy area. I wouldn't send my dog Missy out in those conditions and when I went to put on my parka, I realised that I had left it back in the Nissan Patrol. By this stage I felt more like the shivering shaker than the bearded burbler but there was a job to be done so I walked out into the depths with Foxy.

The mad Tasmanian was as happy as Larry casting his fly into the hurricane and sure enough his fly was slammed as he twitched it back through the waves. Maybe he was right–the trout didn't seem to mind the weather at all! This was a good fish too and it really went to town, jumping all over the place and boring for the bottom. This was a prime specimen, olive green on the back and beautifully spotted with black heavy dots. The jaw was hooked and the back was so wide that Foxy had trouble getting his hand around it.

This particular lake has a very good head of trout in it, so most anglers, including John, kill a percentage of those that they catch. The chances of this fish living to fight another day looked remote, but it had given us such a run for our money I thought it deserved a bit of luck. After we extricated it from my net, we also realised that it was foul-hooked in the middle of the forehead, and that was another reason to let it go. Actually we had almost as much fun getting this fish into the net as we did in catching it–I nearly fell into the water laughing at Foxy tangling his net up in knots so bad, that he couldn't fit the fish in. Of course, I bagged him unmercifully about this, and then tangled my own net as well! That's what fishing is all about–a couple of mates fishing in atrocious conditions and having a ball anyway.

There is a lesson here for anglers visiting Tasmania. When the weather packs up and the more popular methods such as fishing a dry fly for rising fish, or polaroiding for cruisers, are out of the question, don't give up and head back to the shack. Fish often take a fly more aggressively in rough weather and they are more comfortable feeding in a good wave. The water is often slightly mucky after a bit of wind as well and this means that the fish aren't frightened by anglers as readily.

When bad weather hits, shorten your leader to about 2.7m, put on a simple wet fly such as a Mrs Simpson, or a Fur fly like the one Foxy used on our Sorell session, and keep casting. Heavier outfits from about 6 weight to 8 weight are the easiest to use under adverse conditions, so they are the ones to go for. A quick strip retrieve usually works well and lets you cover plenty of ground. When you do catch a fish don't be too hasty to leave the area where you achieved the success. Trout are always looking for tucker and if there is enough food to attract one fish, it is very likely that others will have discovered the larder as well. You can also expect to catch some big fish in Tassie. If you are fishing in the rough stuff, trout are unlikely to notice a heavy leader, so you can use one of 3 to 4kg line. This way, when you hook the big one, it will stay connected after that first frantic run.

Tasmania is a great place to fish and even in the crook weather it can be both productive and fun. Next time, I won't leave my jacket in the Nissan, and I might have a bit more faith when Foxy asks me to wade out into the middle of the lake in a hurricane!

FACT BOX
Foxy and the freezing trout

ROD: 6–9 weight Sage.
REEL: Medium fly reel capable of holding plenty of backing.
LINE: Floating weight forward size 6–9.
BAIT: Small Fur fly.
DANGEROUS FEATURES: None.
TIME OF YEAR: Summer.
LOCATION: Lake Sorell, central Tasmania.

'GOODAY MATE. IT'S JUST ME, REX HUNT FROM CHANNEL 7'S
"REX HUNT'S FISHING ADVENTURES", GOIN' ON A BIT OF A CRUISE WITH
THE LITTLE LADY TO SHOW HER THE SIGHTS. NO NEED TO GET UP.
AND THANK YOUR MOTHER FOR THE RABBITS.' *(Alex Julius)*

LYNNE STRUCK THE JACKPOT WITH THIS BEAUTY CAUGHT ON THE
SENSATIONAL SHIMANO CHRONARCH BAITCASTER. ALLIGATOR RIVER BARRA
SEEM TO JUMP BETTER THAN MOST, BUT THEN AGAIN I RECKON I COULD JUMP
OVER THE MCG IF I THOUGHT ONE OF THOSE ROTTEN CROCS MIGHT GRAB ME.
THEN IT WOULD *DEFINITELY* BE YIBBIDA YIBBIDA, THAT'S ALL FOLKS. *(Alex Julius)*

Rex and Lynne on the Alligator

IT'S NOT OFTEN THAT YOU CAN MIX BUSINESS WITH PLEASURE, BUT WHEN YOU CAN TAKE YOUR WIFE, WHO ALSO HAPPENS TO BE YOUR BEST MATE, TO WORK—WELL, IT JUST DOESN'T GET MUCH BETTER! THE SOUTH ALLIGATOR RIVER SYSTEM IS HOME TO THE BARRAMUNDI AND IT IS JUST A MARVELLOUS PLACE TO VISIT. IT HAS TAKEN A WHILE FOR THE MESSAGE TO GET THROUGH, BUT YOU DON'T HAVE TO BE A BLOKE TO ENJOY THE GREAT PASTIME OF FISHING IN THE NORTH.

My wife Lynne is not a fanatical fishing maniac to the extent that I am, but she does love to be up north chasing barramundi. If you have a companion who is an occasional fisher person and you want them to have the best possible time on the water, it pays to devote some attention to the type of tackle they will use.

The very best gear for fishing northern rivers and creeks is, without doubt, the baitcaster outfit. On this trip I was rigged with state of the art equipment—a Loomis IMX graphite pistol-grip rod and a Shimano Chronarch reel. This type of gear does take a certain amount of practice to master, so newcomers often have more fun and are more successful using a threadline outfit. This type of reel, commonly known as an egg beater, is easy to control and cast with a minimum of instruction and Lynne clicked with that system right from the start.

There are also many different lures around to throw at barra but this time we were using some of the new Stumpjumpers. These lures are made in Australia and they have a couple of novel features such as removable bibs and barbless trebles. Most of us bend down the barbs on our barra hooks with pliers before we head north, but when you buy a Stumpjumper this tedious little job has been done for you. The company uses top quality Eagle Claw hooks that come straight out of the box without barbs.

There are a number of advantages to using barbless hooks. The first one is that they come out of anglers much easier than the barbed variety will! The other advantage is that they go into barramundi much easier. This might sound hard to believe but pulling bumpy barbs into fish is harder than sliding in smooth steel. The really big payoff that comes with the barbless jobs is the ease with which they can be removed from a fish so that it can be released with a minimum of fuss. Once you have faith in the barbless system you wouldn't fish any other way for barra.

The bibs on these lures can be changed easily by bending them and pulling them out of the lure. The bibs come in different colours and in both shallow and deep-running options. The system is neat and effective and the bibs themselves are as tough as hell.

When you are fishing for barra you need to cast accurately. These fish just love deep cover and when they are holed up in the dark recesses of a big snag your lure has to really ring that doorbell before they come out to play. The best thing you can do before you head north on a barra expedition is to practise casting at a target on your back lawn. That way, when you hit barra territory you will be able to make the best of your opportunities.

Through my show I have had the opportunity to fish with some top barramundi anglers so I can pass on a few tips that will make things easier for you when the time comes for your first trip. Persistence is a great asset for a barra fisher–these fish often take a bit of waking up and there is a tendency for young players to throw a few casts in the general direction of a likely snag and then move on. The big trick is to assume that any likely spot does have a couple of fish in residence and to really plaster it with well-directed casts. Sometimes it takes one cast to generate action but often you have to fire in thirty or forty casts before the fish wake up and have a go. I have already mentioned accuracy, but a lure that lands 10cm from a snag is much more likely to be hit than a cast that lands 60cm away. You have to practise that casting and persevere when you are fishing.

Lynne and I had to work hard up on the Alligator because the fish seemed to be in a doggy mood—they just didn't seem fired up at all. Lynne kept casting away with her egg beater outfit and eventually she hooked a beautiful tarpon on a soft plastic lure. This fish jumped all over the place as most members of the tarpon tribe do and it certainly allowed us to show that a spinning reel is capable of doing the job on smaller species up north.

It wasn't in the script to have my wife catch all the fish but, to tell the truth, I was loving every minute of it. There really aren't any restraints on who should go fishing and the game doesn't need a macho image. Everyone can have fun with a fishing rod—it is one game where women or kids or even big kids like me can have fun.

Kakadu is just such a marvellous place to be. This was a very relaxing session as far as I was concerned and right at the end of the day I even caught a barra. I will admit that it wasn't all that large, but it was a barra! Life is very short and if you get the chance to fish with your family, go for it!

FACT BOX

Rex and Lynne on the Alligator

ROD: G. Loomis pistol grip, Shimano spinning rod.
REEL: Shimano Chronarch, Shimano egg beater.
LINE: 6kg monofilament.
LURES: Stumpjumper lure. Soft plastic scrounger lure.
DANGEROUS FEATURES: Cutting spike on gill cover of barramundi.
TIME OF YEAR: Autumn.
LOCATION: Kakadu National Park, Northern Territory.

HAL HARVEY HAS GOT A LOT TO ANSWER FOR, PERCHING ME ON
ONE OF THOSE UNCOMFORTABLE TRIPOD CONTRAPTIONS WHILE THE TIDE
CAME IN AND I COULDN'T MOVE UNTIL IT WENT OUT AGAIN. I SUPPOSE IT
WOULDN'T HAVE BEEN TOO BAD IF WE CAUGHT SOME FISH, BUT THEY WERE
ABOUT AS HARD TO FIND AS ANY OTHER DOPES LIKE US SITTING OUT IN
THE MIDDLE OF THE OCEAN. *(Ron D'Raine)*

Torture in the west

*I'VE DONE SOME STRANGE THINGS TO BRING YOU FOLKS
OUT THERE A LOOK AT FISHING AROUND AUSTRALIA, BUT
BEING STRUNG UP ON A RACK AND SUSPENDED ABOVE
THE WATER WITH THE TIDE COMING IN JUST HAS TO BE
PAST A JOKE! I RECKON HAL HARVEY HAD A BET ON
WITH HIS MATES AND SET OUT TO MAKE THE OLD
BEARDED BURBLER LOOK LIKE A WALLY! FAIR DINKUM, BY
THE TIME I HAD FINISHED A SESSION ON THE RACK YOU
COULD HAVE STUCK A 12\0 TUNA HOOK RIGHT THROUGH
MY LEFT CHEEK AND I WOULDN'T HAVE FELT A THING!
NEXT TIME HAL RINGS ME WITH A SUGGESTION FOR THE
SHOW, I'M GOING TO TELL HIM I AM PLAYING GOLF.*

The idea of tripod fishing is to take a purpose-built aluminium platform out onto the reef at low tide and then to sit suspended over the water as the tide comes in. In theory this puts you high and dry out there, so you can fish in water that could not normally be reached by shore-fishermen at high tide. The catch is that you have to wait until *low* tide before you can leave and go home. What happens if you get one of those major calls of nature in the meantime I am not sure!

Hal told me that this sport actually has a good track record for safety. There has only been one recorded death, and that involved a bloke going off the edge of the reef at night. Apparently the guy couldn't swim at all so I would have to think that he wasn't too bright. If you play by the rules and check your sea conditions first, I can see that the system could be very productive. I certainly wouldn't be keen to try it on a reef at night though.

We didn't exactly set the world on fire during this particular session as far as catching fish went but we had plenty of fun. The most common fish caught over here on tripods would probably be herring, but you could catch whiting or squid as well if you were in the right place. Hal seemed to have taken me to the world capital for rock cod and catching a horde of them was right on the cards whether we wanted them or not. Getting the hooks out of spiky rock cod while you are tied to some shaky scaffolding is one of the big challenges in fishing. We did manage to catch some herring as well, but for me the main interest in the session was the novelty of the whole operation. Come to think of it, if I did buy one of these contraptions I could take it into the crowd at the MCG and call the footy from on top of it!

FACT BOX

Torture in the west

ROD: Medium spinning.

REEL: Medium egg beater.

LINE: 4kg.

HOOKS: Size 6–1 long shank.

BAIT: Squid.

SPECIAL EQUIPMENT: Tripod.

DANGEROUS FEATURES: Falling off tripod!!

TIME OF YEAR: Summer.

LOCATION: Perth, Western Australia.

NOW I'VE SEEN THE LOT. I'VE HEARD THAT BANANAS ARE BAD LUCK ON A
BOAT BUT WHAT ABOUT WHEN THE BOAT *IS* A BANANA?
YOUNG TIM HARRAWAY PROVED THAT BANANAS AND BOATING *DO* MIX BY
LANDING A WHOPPER HINZE DAM BASS. *(David Green)*

Bass trolling with David Green

THE AUSTRALIAN BASS IS ONE OF THE BEST SPORTFISH
GOING AND SEEING THEM STOCKED IN OTHERWISE
UNPRODUCTIVE WATERS IS A GREAT THING.
ON THIS TRIP TO THE GOLD COAST, DAVID GREEN
SHOWED ME A FEW TRICKS OF THE BASS TROLLING TRADE
ON THE HINZE DAM AND SNEAKING AROUND IN
HIS SCANOE WITH AN ELECTRIC MOTOR ON THE
TRANSOM WAS A REAL EYE-OPENER.

This impoundment is surrounded by lush green forest and is a very restful place. Steep tree-covered ranges form a rugged backdrop to the scene and green reeds and grasses carpet the ground right to the water's edge. The water itself is clear and teeming with shrimp and small fish which the bass hammer with a vengeance. Two years ago there were no fish there apart from a few catfish and it is only through the work of a dedicated group of locals that bass were successfully stocked. The fish are now fat and healthy and the fishing is terrific.

I must admit I was a bit sceptical when Greenie showed me our fishing boat because the last time I saw anything like it was when I watched *Deliverance* at the movies. Dave assured me that we wouldn't run into any hillbillies or giant rapids so we loaded up the gear and hooked up the electric motor. Actually, sitting in the big Scanoe was very pleasant. Powered by electricity, we slid over the surface quietly and easily. No fumes, no noise and a beautiful view to look at while we trolled. We weren't far from Surfers Paradise and I was starting to think that this was Fishers Paradise.

It didn't take long for us to strike paydirt either. David's rod buckled over and a nice fish took line in short bursts. The smooth drag rapidly wore the fish down though and it was soon beside the Scanoe. The fish had taken a deep-diving lure fished just over the top of a weed-bed. This was a fairly solid Australian bass but David explained that it had probably only been in the dam for two years. This is almost double the growth rate that you would expect from a fish in a normal wild environment. It just goes to show what a plentiful food supply and an abundance of good shelter can do for fish. According to the good doctor, this fish could double its present weight again in another two years.

It was a pleasure to watch Greenie handling the bass with kid gloves because the only way we are going to guarantee good fishing for the future is to look after individual fish and return them to the water in mint condition. Bass cannot spawn in artificial environments such as Hinze Dam because they don't have access to brackish water. These fish need a certain salinity content before they can breed. This factor means that releasing impoundment bass to be re-caught makes a lot of sense.

The fish from this dam are just bursting with life–they fight like crazy and they are built like Charles Bronson. They are about as good a small sportfish as you could wish for.

Now, my mate Greenie is a bit dubious about kissing fish, but after a bit of persuasion he gave this one the big smooch and slid it back into the water. I keep hammering the point, but fish as good as these are just too valuable to be caught only once.

The gear that I use for trolling bass in impoundments is fairly simple. I favour small overhead outfits called baitcasters. They are great for casting lures accurately into the snags but also offer trouble-free trolling. On this trip I had one outfit spooled with bright yellow line and one spooled with white line. The colour of the line doesn't attract the fish but it does allow you to follow the direction that a fish has taken during a fight. The other reason for using different line colours is to have an instant indicator of which lure is on which outfit. It is only a small factor but it helps in the overall scheme of trolling.

Many of the bass that we target in impoundments seem to hang around weed-beds and I suppose that they do it because there is plenty of tucker around the weeds and plenty of good hiding spots as well if they feel threatened. The main object of the trolling game is to find the particular weed-beds that the fish are using and to troll lures a couple of feet over the vegetation. There are many lures around that will do the job but most of the effective ones are deep divers. On this expedition with Greenie, I was using Stumpjumper lures. These lures have replaceable bibs and you have the choice of shallow or deep options. Sometimes fish will feed over shallow weeds and then you need to troll shallow runners.

Once you find a lure that runs at the right depth, you have to work out a speed that the fish will respond to. To get a rough idea of a speed that suits a particular lure, it is simply a matter of trolling the lure a couple of feet off the rod tip and watching it for a few minutes. If the lure wriggles with plenty of action and doesn't spin or fly out of the water, you can then drop it back to trolling distance. Depending on the conditions, bass may hit slowly trolled offerings or they might prefer something that darts through the water quickly. It pays to experiment on the day. When you start trolling in the morning always give the fish a choice between lures that are running close to your boat or further away, and try to include a couple of different colours in the spread as well. These fish are notoriously fussy but if you give them as many choices as possible they will eventually fall for something.

I was daydreaming and watching the forest glide by when I was rudely awakened by a hard-hitting bass. The fish grabbed a little Stumpjumper that I imagined was wriggling along just over one of the weed-beds. This fish was slightly smaller than the first one and must have come from a later liberation. There was no doubt about the condition factor, these fish are as fat as mud. So far we had only taken bass but there are other fish in Hinze Dam. Apart from the indigenous catfish there are yellowbelly, silver perch and Mary River cod. These three species have not been in the dam long enough to have reached a size that interests anglers yet, but there is certainly a bonanza just around the corner. In another year or two things are going to be hot around the old Hinze Dam and I hope that I might be around to show you just how big the fish have grown.

Most bass anglers are prone to carrying enormous tackle boxes around to accommodate the three million lures they carry, so I am a bit worried about my old mate Greenie. The pay for Queensland doctors must be just awful because poor old Dr Green carries all his lures on a very battered and torn hat. Come to think of it, even the hat is a bit of a give away as to the Green family fortunes! I will be circulating a petition to have Greenie's pay increased, but in the meantime if somebody has a tackle box out there to spare, please let me know!

GREENIE'S FIRST BASS OF THE DAY WAS IN GREAT SHAPE AND WEIGHED ABOUT A KILO. ALL OF THE HINZE DAM FISH ARE IN PERFECT CONDITION AND PUT UP A GREAT FIGHT INDICATING THAT THIS DAM IS JUST BURSTING WITH LIFE.

(David Green)

FACT BOX

Bass trolling with David Green

ROD: Light baitcaster.

REEL: Small overhead Shimano Chronarch.

LINE: 4kg monofilament.

RIG: 4kg line straight through to lure.

LURES: Deep diving Rapalas.

DANGEROUS FEATURES: Cutting spike on gill cover.

TIME OF YEAR: Summer.

LOCATION: Hinze Dam.

THIS LITTLE BONITO WAS CAUGHT OFF SYDNEY HEADS AND PUT UP A GREAT
FIGHT BEFORE IT WAS LANDED, COPPED A FULL-ON REX HUNT SMACKEROO ON
THE CHOPS AND WAS RELEASED TO FIGHT ANOTHER DAY.

(Steve Starling)

Lucky dip - Sydney style

FISHING THE DEEP REEFS OFF SYDNEY IS ALWAYS A LUCKY DIP BUT THAT IS WHAT KEEPS TAKING US BACK. THIS TIME STEVE STARLING AND I WENT FIRST CLASS ON THE CHARTER BOAT FISHFINDER WITH SKIPPER TONY DAVIS. FOR ONCE THE WEATHER WAS KIND AND WE CAUGHT A VARIETY OF TASTY FISH INCLUDING THE FAMOUS JOHN DORY. I HAD TO PHYSICALLY RESTRAIN STEVE FROM EATING THE DORY ON THE SPOT, BUT LATER ON WE TURNED THE CATCH INTO A MEMORABLE SEAFOOD FEAST!

We started our trip from Balmain Peninsula in Sydney Harbour and the view on the way out, even before we started fishing, was worth the price of admission. This just has to be one of the prettiest harbours in the world and to see it from the deck of a charter boat early in the morning is a privilege. We went under the old coat hanger, right past the Opera House and the tall towers of the central business district, and straight out through the Heads. Fantastic! On the way out to the grounds Steve told me about a special fish he was particularly keen to catch on this trip. His eyes were wide and he had to keep wiping the drool from his mouth, so I knew that the long-finned sea perch had to be a spectacular table fish. If one made it on to the deck I didn't give it much chance of a happy release and a kiss from my right hand man. Not that I am trying to say that Steve has a reputation for being a bit savage on the tooth or anything, but I have heard it said that a tooth brush is the only thing ever to have actually made the trip both in and out of the Starling mouth!

The big power cat made the trip out an absolute breeze and it only took about 45 minutes for us to reach our destination on one of the seventy fathom reefs. It is a bit of an epic to fish 24km out to sea in an amateur boat unless you are very experienced and own an expensive rig. Charter boats offer an easy and relatively inexpensive way to tackle deep water bottom bouncing. Some of you folks are probably already moaning about seasickness, but that shouldn't stop you unless you are a chronic sufferer. Even Steve Starling, who writes about fishing for a living, admits to having bouts of the dreaded deep sea heaves. In most cases the problem can be managed by taking a pill and watching what you eat before your trip. It is a good idea to keep off the grog and to make sure that you get a good night's sleep before a deep water expedition. Watching the horizon, or the hazy line of the land, if you can see any, can also be a help. The main thing is not to give up on the deep sea stuff too easily. Sometimes it takes a few trips to settle in. On this trip we didn't have anything to worry about because there was no swell at all and only a light chop from the north.

When you are bottom bouncing it is no good beating around the bush. You have to tie on a serious sinker that weighs about three quarters of a pound on the old scale, and get down where the fish are. Seventy fathoms works out to be about 130m and that is a long way down. Simple rigs seem to work best for this type of fishing and I was using my favourite Paternoster rig this time. All you need to make this rig is a length of 24kg line with a sinker on one end and two equidistant droppers with 4\0 hooks tied to them in the middle. Hooks without kirbs, that is straight hooks, are often used for deep reef fishing because they have less tendency to twist on the way to the bottom. Again, this is not a vital point, but in fishing, every little detail you can fine-tune helps to catch you more fish. The same care should be applied to rigging baits. Try and make your baits as symmetrical as possible so as to avoid line-twist and tangles.

I baited up with a half pilchard and a full aero squid and started the whole shebang on its way to the bottom. The spool on my reel seemed to revolve forever, but eventually it stopped and I was down amongst the fish. Steve had also snuck his bait over the side and he was the first to get stuck into a fish. It really is a lottery out there and there is no way you can tell what you have on the line until the hard work is done and you have cranked the fish up to the surface. Steve was working up a sweat, but the fish was getting closer.

When the fish had nearly reached the surface, the line went decidedly slack. If this happens to you, keep on winding because it probably just means that the decrease in pressure has blown up the fish's air bladder. Once this happens, the fish will float to the surface and bring the heavy lead with him. This first fish turned out to be a blubber lip morwong. According to Steve, these are great table fish, so this one went straight into the ice slurry. We didn't give this fish the Rex Hunt kiss because we had just pulled him up from the depths and it is unlikely that he would have recovered had we released him. Some fish can handle vast pressure differences, but as a general rule you might as well eat anything that you pull up from deep water. The only way to practise sound conservation when you are deep fishing is to stop when you have enough fish.

While we were removing the hook from old rubber lips, I noticed Steve had a really sexy rig on the end of his line. It looked as though Tina Turner had lost a stack of earrings and Steve had found them. His hooks were more like salt water flies and they flashed in the sun like little jewels. Actually the Japanese have been using rigs such as these for years and they work very well for bottom fishing. The extra flash and movement of these cunning rigs does attract more fish. In the past the commercial Japanese rigs available here have been a bit fragile for Aussie fish but now there are home grown versions around that are quite tough. The rig that Steve was using was made by a bloke up in south Queensland and going by the results that Steve was getting with his gear, I would say that he will have plenty of business in the future. Fair dinkum though, it is a bit tough when these young whippersnappers have to resort to handing out rotten old pilchards to the bearded burbler, and then sneak new fancy rigs onto their own lines!

The next fish to surface from the lucky dip was a fair-sized trevally. Steve was making eating noises again, and I don't blame him. Fresh trevally is an underrated food fish and both of us like to eat them. Even if you are looking for a good honest fish to feed the family from the local market, trevally are a top choice. It is fairly easy to remove the bones from these fish if you have kids to feed, and the flavour of the flesh is great.

So far we had some top eating fish but this time we really hit the jackpot. After a bit more grunting and groaning from Steve, a great big John Dory lay wallowing on the surface. Now, if these weird looking things aren't the best eating fish in the sea, they must come close, so when Steve went to lift the fish in and the hook fell out, the look on his face was priceless. Talk about a panic to find a net! Really it was too easy folks–just like taking a mark at the MCG–I reached out the long Rex Hunt arm and lifted dinner into the boat. Would you take a look at that! The only thing I have ever seen with a mouth as big as mine! These fish are actually savage predators even

'HOWDY FOLKS. I'M REX HUNT...AND YOU'RE NOT!
WELCOME TO SYDNEY...ANYONE FOR SASHIMI?' FISHING WITH A FEW FRIENDS
AT LADY MACQUARIE'S CHAIR ON *MAAAGNIFICENT* SYDNEY HARBOUR.
(Steve Starling)

though they aren't fast movers. They just sneak along and then the big mouth shoots out and yibbida yibbida, that's all folks!

Steve had actually caught a small fish and the old Dory had gone in for the free meal. The small fry had flared out his spikes and fins and jammed in the big Dory gob. That was all the grip that Steve needed to haul him to the top. These Dories are magnificent fish, with white lines, flaring long fins, and the identifying 'thumb' mark supposedly put on to the fish by JC. When you taste one, you will know why he picked the Dory as his favourite tucker!

I was really starting to appreciate this lucky dip fishing and the best was yet to come. We finally caught the fish that Steve was all fired up about. Yes folks, the old bearded burbler came good and pulled up a ripper long-finned sea perch just as the sun sank down over Sydney. I thought that Steve was going to swim home and start cooking the fish before we fired up the big outboards, and there was even some talk of sashimi on the way home, so I had to guard the catch from one of the fiercest fish fangs on the ocean all the way back to port, but it was eventually worth it and we dined in style.

There is no doubt about it, charter boats such as *Fishfinder* make fishing out wide easy and enjoyable and Steve and I had a great day fishing in the seventy fathom lucky dip.

FACT BOX
Lucky dip - Sydney style

ROD: Whippy tip, stiff butt.
REEL: Medium Shimano overhead.
LINE: 10kg.
RIG: Paternoster.
HOOKS: 2/0 to 6/0.
SINKERS: Heavy.
BAIT: Squid and pilchard.
TIME OF YEAR: Autumn.
LOCATION: Seventy Fathom Reef, off Sydney.

CATCHING BAIT TOWNSVILLE STYLE. THE FIRST THROW SAW ABOUT
1.5KG OF PRAWNS IN THE NET. AND IF YOU DON'T CATCH ANY FISH ON 'EM,
THEY ARE *DEEEEEELICIOUS* EATING FOLKS.

MY GUIDE, TONY JETSON OF NORTH AUSTRALIAN SPORTFISHING IN
TOWNSVILLE. TONY'S ON FIRST NAME TERMS WITH THE FISH IN THESE PARTS,
HAVING CAUGHT MOST OF THEM AND THEN THROWN 'EM BACK.

Murray River monsters

QUEENSLAND'S MURRAY RIVER USUALLY DOES PRODUCE
TOP FISHING BUT THIS TIME THE ONLY MONSTERS WE
CAUGHT WERE MEAN, UGLY, AND POISONOUS! SOMETIMES
YOU CAN HAVE THE BEST GUIDE IN THE WORLD ON A
GREAT RIVER SYSTEM, BUT WHEN THE FISHING SCENE
SHUTS DOWN, THINGS CAN BE VERY TOUGH. THEY WERE
SO TOUGH ON THIS TRIP THAT I HAD TO EAT THE BAIT!

The Murray River is situated about midway between Cairns
and Townsville and it has no connection with that other
Murray further south. This river has some of the biggest stands
of mangroves you have ever seen in your life in its lower reaches
and normally it has plenty of fish to offer visiting anglers. Tony
Jetson operates a guiding operation called North Australian
Sportfishing out of Townsville and he probably knows as much
about the area as anyone. King salmon, barramundi, javelin fish,
mangrove jacks and fingermark bream all inhabit these waters and
on this trip we intended to target them with one of the best baits
in the north–live prawns.

Tony is a gun man with a cast net and that is just as well,
because that is the best method of collecting a mess of live
banana prawns. We stopped at a likely looking mud bank and
Tony coiled up the net, draped it over his arm, whirled around
like a ballet dancer, and threw it over a school of prawns. Pretty
to watch! The first throw saw about a kilo and a half of prawns
meshed in the net, so the bait problem was solved in about five
minutes. The prawns were carefully put into the live bait tank
to swim around happily for the rest of the day. I must admit that
those prawns looked very tasty, but duty called, so they man-

aged to stay off the Rex Hunt food list and on the fish-bait list!

The fishing hole was about 3km from the bait gathering spot, so it was a case of hold your hat and hang on while Tony fed some petrol to the outboard. He doesn't call his boat *Hyperspace* for nothing, so it didn't take long to arrive at the hot hole! Tony explained that we were fishing in a hole about 6m deep along an undercut bank. There is an eddy in this hole and fish like to hang around in it, both when the tide is running in, and when it runs the other way.

Tony used a simple Paternoster rig tied from 18kg monofilament with a 15cm dropper. The favoured hook was a Mustad 37140 wide gape. These hooks look a bit weird, but they are made from thin diameter wire and penetrate very easily. The prawn is hooked once through the back and cast out into the hole. After that, it is just a case of waiting. On this trip, it was a case of waiting a lot!

The first taker was an aggressive little mangrove jack. He just couldn't wait to get his fangs into my live prawn, and I do mean fangs! These fish are efficient killers and this one had power to burn even though he was only a little bloke. If you ever make it up north and tangle with a few jacks be dead careful when you are retrieving lures or hooks from their jaws. Use pliers to be on the safe side because one mistake can mean a bad injury and a ruined trip. Tony was happy to release this jack and it is a credit to him that he encourages 100 per cent catch and release. This is definitely the way to go if any guiding operation is to succeed.

My next bite felt weird from the start and I didn't have a clue as to what was chewing on my prawn. When my sluggish opponent finally came to the boat I just about jumped out of the other side. I have seen a few ugly things in my day but this thing made the Elephant Man look like Tom Cruise! What is brown, warty, covered in poisonous spikes, and gives you the evil eye while you are trying to take the hook out of it? A devil fish, of course, and very aptly named too. This was the most awful fish I have ever caught and I never want to see another one!

This was turning into one of those days; the next fish that I caught had a head on it almost as bad as the devil fish. This was a northern pike eel. It was about 1.5m long with teeth like a barracuda. I had a fair idea that these things are a bit of a worry when Tony wouldn't even let it near the boat. He cut the line while the pike eel was still at a safe distance. I was a bit worried about casting again in case I reeled in Phyllis Diller!

Sometimes in fishing things just go dead, and this time they had. There is not a lot you can do about it except to make the best of what is on offer. I had been keeping a good eye on those lovely fresh prawns all day and at last the moment had come. The fishing was shot, but the old bearded burbler whipped the shells off a couple of prawns and yibbida yibbida folks, they were down the hatch! *Deelicious!*

FACT BOX

Murray River monsters

ROD: Pistol grip.
REEL: Light Shimano Chronarch overhead.
LINE: 6kg.
BAIT: Live prawns.
DANGEROUS FEATURES: Spikes on devil fish. Teeth on pike eel and mangrove jack.
TIME OF YEAR: Autumn.
LOCATION: Murray River near Cairns, Queensland.

STREWTH, IT WAS COLD. I COULD HAVE SWORN I SAW A BRASS MONKEY
WANDERING AROUND LOOKING FOR A WELDER. AND TO ADD INSULT TO INJURY,
FOXY HELD THE TROUT IN FRONT OF MY NOGGIN AND I HARDLY
GET IN THE PICTURE.

Drift spinning with "The Fox" on Lake Sorell

THERE IS MORE THAN ONE WAY TO SKIN A CAT, AND THERE IS MORE THAN ONE WAY TO CATCH A TROUT. MY OLD MATE JOHNNY FOX KNOWS ALL THE TRICKS IN TASSIE AND HE TOOK US ONTO ONE OF HIS FAVOURITE LAKES TO SHOW US HOW TO DRIFT SPIN FOR THE ELUSIVE BROWN TROUT.

I have been spinning for trout for more years than I care to remember and I guess many of you have put in some time with a spinning rod as well. Drift spinning is something new to me and I was keen to try it with Foxy. As soon as we launched the boat, I could see that the day was perfect for what we had in mind. You could probably say that it was a typical Tasmanian summer's day. That's right, freezing bloody cold, with a fair wind blowing! It was also cloudy and grey. You could just see the surrounding hills through the damp mist. No wonder these pommy trout love the place, they probably think they are still in England! It is still a beautiful place though, and now that I have been there a few times I really enjoy fishing there.

The conditions actually were perfect because trout love to feed in a bit of a wave and we needed the breeze to push the boat across the lake so we could cover plenty of different ground. Drift spinning is a very simple technique. You select an area that you feel will be productive, let the boat drift with the wind and start casting lures and retrieving them. When you think about it, the method has a lot going for it. For a start, it is absolutely quiet–there are no clunking oars, no roaring outboards and no slap slap slapping of an aluminium hull banging into the waves. It is also cheap—you don't use any fuel at all while you are drifting. Once you are drifting over a productive area there are a few basic tricks to learn before you can master the technique.

Long casting is one of the things that puts the odds in your favour when you are drift fishing. A long cast means a long retrieve and that allows a trout to follow your lure long enough to make up his mind to strike it. On a short cast a fish will often see the lure, start to chase it and then see the boat and turn away.

Long easy casting starts the moment you select your gear. You need a light spinning rod with plenty of flick in the tip and a good quality spinning reel to balance it. Always use the best line you can afford and make sure that you fill the spool on your reel almost to the lip. Your choice of lures will also affect the distance that you achieve. Heavier lures such as Tassie Devils and Lofty's Cobras cast like bullets and are proven fish killers. My favourite Tiger Devon also has plenty of weight and I like it because it makes plenty of fizz in the water but runs straight and is easy for fish to wrap their mouths around. If you do use Devon spinners, make sure that you include a little plastic keel about 60cm from your lure because without one, line twist will be a problem.

Finding productive areas can be a matter of trial and error, or you can take a leaf out of Foxy's book and use a depth sounder to locate shallow reefs in your lake. Foxy uses the sounder to find shallow weedy reefs that rise up out of about 3m of water and then positions the boat so that it drifts over them. This means that the lures are tracking over ground where fish are likely to be feeding. This is the same connection that I run into as I fish all over Australia—find a good weed-bed and the fish won't be far away.

We had only tried a couple of drifts across one of John's Sorell reefs when my little Vibrax lure was absolutely slammed right next to the boat. Tassie trout go berserk when they feel the hook and this one was no exception. He wasn't huge but was in great condition and I had a certain spot in mind for him back at the Rex Hunt den in Melbourne. No, not on the wall—on the barby!

One of the good things about fishing Sorell is that the trout have access to ideal natural spawning conditions. This means that the stocks are continually replenished and the fish need to be culled to some extent to maintain the average size. This is the perfect angling scenario, a fishery where you can take a few for the pan without doing any damage to the fish population.

Foxy was the next to strike and his Devon was walloped by a better fish out in the waves. This one jumped all over the place but eventually we had him at the side of the boat. This is where a lot of fish are lost. Always use a net when you are fishing from a boat because it is the safest way to land a fish and it allows you to release any unwanted ones without damaging them. The best way to do the job is to position the net in the water first and then drag the fish over the top of it. A steady lift with the net should see the fish well and truly caught. I did the job properly for Foxy and we had a typical Tassie brown trout in the boat.

It was great fun doing some drift spinning and I'm sure that I will be doing plenty more of it in the future. I wonder if I could get Foxy to invite me over so that I could try it in the winter. Perhaps we could just cut one of those little holes in the ice and drop our lines through for a bit of ice spinning!

FACT BOX

Drift spinning with 'The Fox' on Lake Sorell

BROWN AND RAINBOW TROUT
ROD: Light whippy spinning.
REEL: Egg beater style Shimano.
LINE: 2kg.
LURES: Devon Minnows and Tassie Devils.
DANGEROUS FEATURES: None.
TIME OF YEAR: Believe it or not, summer!
LOCATION: Lake Sorell, central Tasmania.

YES, IT DOES RUN IN THE FAMILY FOLKS. MY SON MATTHEW WITH
A 4KG RAINBOW TROUT THAT MADE MY ATTEMPTS LOOK PRETTY ORDINARY,
I'LL TELL YOU. I GUESS IT'S MY FAULT FOR TEACHING HIM TOO WELL.

Wall to wall fishing with Terry Shephard

TERRY SHEPHARD ASKED ME TO MEET HIM WHERE
LAKE EILDON MEETS THE GOULBURN RIVER, AND ASKED
IF I WAS SCARED OF HEIGHTS. THAT SEEMED LIKE A
FUNNY THING TO ASK UNTIL I FOUND HIM AND MY SON
MATTHEW PERCHED 9M UP ON A CONCRETE WALL!
THE HEIGHT DIDN'T BOTHER ME AT ALL WHEN I SAW
WHAT THEY HAD BEEN CATCHING.

Lying right next to the wall was a trout that most people would only dream of catching. It was a whopping great rainbow, and if I had to fish from a concrete wall to catch one that size then I figured I had better start learning some concrete tricks. Just to rub salt into the wound Terry pulled up his monster keeper net and showed me more trout than you would see in the Snobs Creek hatchery on a good day!

You just wouldn't believe that there would be fish where we were fishing. Looking up, you could see the vast height of the Eildon Dam wall and the plume of white water splashing out and sliding down the spillway. We were on top of one of the walls forming the square basin that is the start of the Goulburn below the dam. This was a bit like fishing in a concrete tank, but you couldn't argue with the results. The fish are obviously attracted to the well-oxygenated water pouring in, and are keen to swim up the river and congregate in the artificial pool.

Terry is an innovative fisherman and had modified his coarse fishing techniques to make the best of the situation. I hate to tell you folks, but Terry was up to his old tricks again and was up to his armpits in his favourite bait—you guessed it, the dreaded maggots! Here we go again, I thought. When Terry showed how to keep bait in the fridge on my show, I copped so much flak from guardians of the fridge, that my beard went two shades whiter. Fair dinkum, would you give a poor old fisherman a go, Terry!

The baiting method hadn't changed from the way we did it last time, we still put a tiny hook through the thick end of a few creepy crawlers. Make sure that you put it through the thick end, because if you stick the maggot through the thin end, which is the head, it will die. Now the last thing you would want on your hook would be a heap of dead maggots, right? Dead maggots—marvellous, Terry!

When you use the Terry Shephard maggot system, you not only get to stick hooks through them, you get to play with them while you stuff a berley cage full of them. This is the big trick to consistent catches. If you keep casting the rig into the same place, the smell attracts the fish and they remain in the area to feed on the maggots coming out of the berley feeder. When a fish finds your little squirming bunch, it is a case of yibbida yibbida, that's all folks, and it is all over. When you do get a bite it pays to strike straight away. Coarse fishing tackle is very sensitive and as soon as you see the slightest indication on the fine tip of your rod, it is time to hit the fish.

I couldn't wait to try my chances in the big pool, so I baited up (through the thick end of course) and heaved the rig into the swirling water. It wasn't long before the old rod-tip gave a couple of telltale twitches and I struck hard and put a bend into my old faithful floppy yellow rod. My fish wasn't as big as some of the whoppers in the keeper net, but it was proof that attention to detail and planning does improve your catch. The constant pressure of the soft rod wore the fish down fairly quickly and soon it was flopping on the surface. It was at this stage that I noticed a slight problem – the fish was 9m down, I was on top of a dirty big concrete wall, and I was using very skinny 1.2kg line!

The boys finally showed me the answer to my predicament, and I must admit I was impressed. Terry certainly thinks a lot about his fishing and had come up with a novel solution to the problem. He pulled out a contraption that appeared to be a modified crab pot. This gadget was rigged on a strong cord and was designed to be lowered into the water next to a fish that had been played out. When everything is ready, the fish is led over the mouth of the net and the net is pulled up by hand with the fish inside it. At least that is the theory! This thing worked brilliantly and easily and I could see that it could work well in a variety of situations. It only took a minute or so and my little brown trout was safely at the top of the wall.

We had plenty of fish already and this particular one looked full of life, so I decided he should have the big hairy kiss instead of the trip to the frying pan! Letting him go from the top of a high wall probably wasn't ideal, but fish are dropped from low flying planes to seed remote lakes, so I thought that it was worth a try. In the end, my little trout made a fairly good landing and I think he would have survived the trip.

Well, I have been on some strange fishing expeditions but this one was certainly different! Fishing under a dam wall, in a square concrete hole, from the top of a high concrete wall, and using baby blowflies for bait! After this one, I think that the old bearded burbler has just about seen it all!

FACT BOX

Wall to wall fishing with Terry Shephard

BROWN AND RAINBOW TROUT
ROD: Very long and whippy with fine tip.
REEL: Egg beater, light Shimano.
LINE: 1.2kg.
RIG: No 18 hook and berley feeder.
HOOKS: Small.
BAIT: Baby blowies!
DANGEROUS FEATURES: Falling off wall.
TIME OF YEAR: Winter.
LOCATION: Eildon Weir, near Melbourne, Victoria.

HERE'S THE OLD PORTLAND PIER FISHING LEGEND HIMSELF, JOHN CONSIDINE,
WITH A WAREHOU, KNOWN LOCALLY AS A HADDOCK. GET A LOAD OF THAT
NOGGIN. IT LOOKS LIKE IT'S DONE NINE ROUNDS WITH MIKE TYSON. AND THE
WAREHOU DOESN'T LOOK REAL GOOD EITHER. THANK YOU VERY MUCH.

On the Portland Pier with John Considine

IF YOU LIKE PIER FISHING, PORTLAND HARBOUR JUST HAS TO BE A TOP SPOT BECAUSE THERE ARE MORE PIERS THERE THAN IN SAN FRANCISCO. THERE ARE BOTH SIMPLE ROCK WALLS AND BIG OCEAN WHARVES THAT SERVICE HUGE SHIPS BOUND FOR FOREIGN PORTS. WE WANTED TO SEE JUST WHAT AN ORDINARY FAMILY FISHERMAN COULD EXPECT TO CATCH BY DANGLING A LINE AMONGST THE PYLONS AND THIS HISTORIC LOCATION DIDN'T LET US DOWN.

If you happen to find yourself in Portland, you don't need any fancy gear to go jetty dangling. John and I were using light threadline tackle and even the rigs that we employed were simple ones. I went for my old favourite Paternoster rig with the bottom dropper hanging below the sinker and the top dropper sitting just above it, and John just slid a light ball sinker on to his line and tied a small long-shanked hook to the end of the line. Both these rigs will work well for you and your kids and they are dead simple to make.

The big trick when fishing piers is to dangle your line straight down rather than to trying to cast to the other side of the bay. How often do you see someone busting a gut trying to drop their sinker a hundred yards from the pier, when all the fish are happily living right under the structure? Take a tip from Rex, kids, let the adults do all the huffing and puffing—you just drop your bait over the side and you will be the ones catching fish.

The first fish of the day was not spectacular, but when a family is fishing together, the old slimy mackerel offers plenty of entertainment, and is a commonly caught harbour species. This one darted around a bit and gave me at least a bit of excitement. Apart from being a good fish for kids to catch, the mackerel makes great bait, both dead or alive. They also make terrific fishcakes.

The next fish to hit the deck was a leatherjacket, and this species is also a great staple of wharf fishing all over the country. The six-spined Elvis Presley might not be a pretty specimen, but he is easy for the kids to catch and is very tasty on a plate. All the kids need to fish for leatheries is a small long-shanked hook and a small piece of tough bait such as squid. If there are a few leatherjackets around, introducing a bit of berley to the scene often works wonders. If there is plenty of free tucker floating down, the 'jackets' just seem to keep coming out of the woodwork and the kids can often have a ball and amass a good family feed.

So far Portland had shown us two basic family fish, but it was up to John Considine to hook one of the best jetty battlers around. His rod rattled and thumped and he actually had a hard time keeping this fish away from the piles. John's fish was another common jetty species. Known locally as 'haddock', the warehou is quite a handsome fish that fights hard on a rod and is a fine eating fish. To get the best taste possible from warehou, they should be killed quickly and bled before going straight on ice. This procedure guarantees a fine meal at the end of the day. One interesting feature of the warehou is that it is absolutely covered in slime! This accounts for their common nickname of snotties—perhaps not the most romantic of names, but certainly an accurate one! Warehou will take a wide variety of baits, but they are cannibalistic, so a cube of warehou flesh (preferably without the skin) is a deadly bait.

When the time came for me to do the kiss and release thing I found out about the slime in a big way. The fish just shot out of my hands like a greased banana and hit the water swimming! That would have to be the slickest release ever seen on national television! The bad news was that it took about three weeks to get the snotty stuff out of my beard!

*N*o folks, you're not dreaming. That fish on the right is a whiting, not a white pointer. Uncle Doug Clegg's tackle shop manager, Chris 'Choco' Field, with a haul of whoppers including that 1.85kg monster.

*T*he mudeye (left) is the larval stage of the dragonfly (right). Here, a newly hatched dragonfly dries its wings before taking to the air. *(Steve Starling)*

I'll go to any lengths to find those fish, even if it means chartering a submarine. Leatherjackets ahead! *(Paul B. Kidd)*

*T*he old Elvis Presley fish–the leatherjacket. Just be very careful with that spike.

*M*y sidekick on 'Rex Hunt's Fishing Adventures', Steve Starling, with a superbly coloured jack rainbow trout from Rock Hut Creek in NSW.

(courtesy Steve Starling)

*H*ow's this for a *maaagnificent* John Dory taken from Tony Davis's *Fishfinder* on one of our Sydney visits. *(Steve Starling)*

*A*re there any questions?' In the shadow of the old coathanger. *(Steve Starling)*

Peter Pakula with
a beautifully
conditioned Hinze
Dam bass.
(David Green)

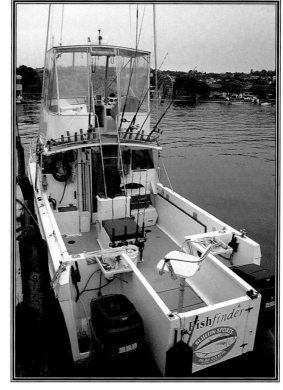

Tony Davis's fabulous
Sydney charter
boat, *Fishfinder*. Tony
looks after the
'Rex Hunt's Fishing
Adventures' team when
we're in Sydney.
(Paul B. Kidd)

*N*ow that's a bit more like it, Greenie. How come you couldn't get me one when I was there? *(courtesy David Green)*

*T*hat man with the mo, our very own Bushy, getting his fly back from a stud rainbow. (*courtesy Bushy*)

'*T*hat doesn't look like the 12 Mile Reef to me, Tony. Can't they make one of those gadgets with writing on it, instead of numbers?' (*Paul B. Kidd*)

*O*ne of 'Rex Hunt's Fishing Adventures' biggest supporters, John Dunphy,
seen here with a whopper red emperor, caught, of course, on his
fabulous Shimano tackle. *(Paul B. Kidd)*

Visiting Portland isn't just about the fishing either–the place is a walking, talking history lesson. Portland was the site of the first settlement in Victoria and there is still feuding going on to decide which family started the whole thing off. In 1836 the Duttons and the Hentys came on the scene and I am not going to be the one to decide between them. If you mention the wrong opinion in front of the wrong family you could be lynched!

If you are looking for an interesting place to visit with the family and you fancy some basic no-fuss fishing, Portland could be the place for you.

FACT BOX

On the Portland Pier with John Considine

ROD: Light and whippy.
REEL: Light egg beater.
LINE: 3kg.
RIG: Paternoster.
HOOKS: Small.
BAIT: Squid.
DANGEROUS FEATURES: None.
TIME OF YEAR: Winter.
LOCATION: Portland, southern Victoria.

FISHING WITH YOUNG LEE RAINER WAS TERRIFIC BUT UNFORTUNATELY
THE WEATHER BEAT US. LEE IS MAKING A CAREER OF FISHING
AND THE FISHING MEDIA, AND IT'S GREAT TO KNOW THAT WE'LL BE LEAVING
THE SPORT IN VERY CAPABLE HANDS. *(Steve Starling)*

Lee Rainer at Rock Hut Creek

ON THIS FISHING TRIP I MET A KEEN YOUNG FLY FISHER HIGH IN THE SNOWY MOUNTAINS AT ROCK HUT CREEK. IT IS GOING TO BE OUR YOUNG PEOPLE WHO TAKE FISHING FORWARD IN THE FUTURE AND I WOULD LIKE MORE OF THEM TO REALISE THAT FLY FISHING IS NOT ONLY A SPORT FOR RICH COLLINS STREET SPECIALISTS. LEE RAINER HAS ALREADY BEEN FISHING FOR A NUMBER OF YEARS AND IS ONLY SEVENTEEN YEARS OLD. IF HE CAN DO IT, SO CAN YOU.

*T*here is also a myth around that fly fishing is a very difficult thing to do. Most young blokes are fairly coordinated and learning to cast a fly rod is simple enough. This game is a bit like golf–it is hard to master, but it isn't hard to learn enough to have some fun.

In recent times the expense of fly fishing has decreased incredibly. It is still possible to spend an arm and a leg on the very best gear, but good basic tackle can be purchased for about $150. This includes rod, reel, and line. Some shops will even tie on a fly on the leader for that money so all you need to add is a trout! When you consider a Super Nintendo game costs around $100, a fly outfit represents terrific value.

Rock Hut Creek is a series of dams on private property near Cooma in New South Wales, and I was fishing along the edge of the main dam with Lee. The weather was freezing cold so there wasn't much surface activity and we were both searching the water with wet flies. This is a good way for youngsters to start their fly careers because it is very similar to searching the water with a spinning lure. The casting is different and the retrieving is as well, but the basic idea of covering likely spots and searching for fish is the same. You just cast the flyline out onto the water and then retrieve it in small jerks until a fish hits it. There is usually no time to worry if a fish decides to take your fly—it is either hooked or not on the first pull.

On Lee's advice I had tied a small Tom Jones fly to the end of my leader, because in this particular dam there were plenty of damsel flies. The Tom Jones is a slim fly that trout often eat in mistake for a damsel and that is just what happened this time. The rod was nearly wrenched out of my hands by a fit rainbow trout. The colours on these impoundment fish are quite spectacular—olive along the back, black-spotted and with a flush of bright crimson down the side—beautiful! The air was still and crisp and all around the lake a light cover of snow mantled the vegetation. Sometimes this job is just magic and I wouldn't swap my life for anyone else's.

Although he loves his fly fishing, Lee is also a keen exponent of spinning and bait fishing, and his intention is to fish with whatever technique gives him the best chance of catching a fish. This seems to be a very well-balanced attitude to the sport of fishing and I would like to see more juniors adopt a similar approach. Lee is a junior Shimano angler and he has spent some time at South West Rocks going through the Shimano angling camp. This program is nurturing juniors around the country and it is great to see one of our biggest tackle companies putting something back into the game.

After a great start in front of the Channel 7 cameras Lee was starting to shake, but it wasn't stage fright, it was the cold. It was tons of fun fishing for rainbows at Rock Hut, but the temperature had fallen through the floor and a session patting the dogs in front of a roaring log fire seemed like a better idea.

If all our juniors are as dedicated to fishing as young Lee Rainer is, I would say that the old bearded burbler can eventually leave the sport in good hands.

FACT BOX

Lee Rainer at Rock Hut Creek

ROD: Loomis No 5 Fly rod.

REEL: 5-6 Flyreel.

LINE: No 5 Weight forward.

RIG: Tapered 2.7m mono leader, 1.8kg tippet.

BAIT: Tom Jones fly.

DANGEROUS FEATURES: None.

TIME OF YEAR: Winter.

LOCATION: Rock Hut Creek,
Monaro,
New South Wales.

Now *THIS* IS WHAT WAS SUPPOSED TO HAPPEN FOLKS. 'REX HUNT'S FISHING
ADVENTURES' REGULAR, ROSS MCCUBBIN, GAFFS A 30KG MULLOWAY FOR
HIS DAD IN THE SOUTHPORT SEAWAY. BUT THE BEST GREENIE COULD MANAGE
FOR US WAS SOME BREAM AND A FANTAIL JACKET. *(David Green)*

Freeway bream at Southport

WELL, WE MIGHT AS WELL HAVE BEEN FISHING IN THE MIDDLE OF A FREEWAY—EVERY FIVE SECONDS OR SO A BOAT OR A HELICOPTER WENT PAST! DR DAVID GREEN HAD SET THE BOAT UP IN THE ENTRANCE TO THE SOUTHPORT ESTUARY SYSTEM AND WHILE WE WERE TRYING TO CATCH A BIG 'JEWIE' OUR BAITS WERE CONTINUALLY MOLESTED BY BREAM. WITH THE 'CHOPPERS', THE BOATS AND THE FISH, THERE CERTAINLY IS A LOT GOING ON IN SOUTH QUEENSLAND!

*A*part from dodging the traffic, David took a lot of care positioning the boat before the anchor went down. This was because we wanted to fish alongside a jewfish highway. There is a pipeline on the bottom of the Broadwater to pump sand from the south side of the seaway to South Stradbroke Island. The pipeline offers the fish shelter from the fast current that rips through the area and they often travel along it. Keen anglers look for the pipe with their depth sounders and position their boats to ambush the fish. There is a lesson for all of us in these tactics—you have to exercise the old brain box if you want to catch fish.

The boat was hanging nicely on the anchor rope and we were roughly over the pipeline. The current was ripping past at about five or six knots, which is very quick, so we only needed a front anchor to keep us steady.

Our main aim was to catch one of the big mulloway, but we also put out some smaller rigs to tempt the winter run bream. The jewfish rigs were heavy duty and complete with sturdy overhead reels full of 10kg line. Live yellowtail are the best baits for the big predators and we had a live bait tank full of them. Jewfish are often tricky to hook so we rigged our baits with two hooks. With this cunning terminal rig, one hook goes through the snout of the yellowtail and one goes through the back near the tail. When you rig any live bait make sure that you don't run the hook through the backbone or the bait will die very quickly. We used simple running sinker rigs for the bream and because of the fast current we used large ball sinkers running to the swivels. We left our traces fairly long (around a metre) so they could waft around enticingly to attract the attention of the bream. The beauty of the running sinker rig is that even when you have to use heavy weights, the bites are easy to feel because the line slides easily through the hole in the sinker–'that's magic, Johnny!'

Our first taker nailed a strip bait on one of my nibble-tip rods and really went to town in the fast current. As we suspected it turned out to be a healthy winter run bream, its belly distended with a load of eggs. It is fantastic to see a waterway that sees so much use still producing quality fish like this one. I gave our bream the Channel 7 smooch and sent it on its way to breed up a few more piscatorial sons and daughters! It was easy to release this fish because I was using a long-shanked hook. These hooks set well in the mouths of fish and it is easy to grasp the long shank and work the hook out with a minimum of stress on the fish. When I use these hooks in estuaries I also add a small piece of red plastic tube that I feel acts as an extra attractor for the fish.

Something must have been working well because the light rods kept on producing bream at regular intervals throughout the session. The jewfish, however, were absent! I like to stir Greenie up when I go to Queensland, so I caught a fantail leatherjacket just to keep him on his toes. David had never heard of a fantail being caught in the Broadwater, but then again, I'm Rex Hunt and he's not! These things are a weird-looking fish wherever you catch them and I enjoy showing folks some of our more exotic species.

During a quiet spell I quizzed David as to just why there is so much air traffic in the area and he explained that most of the helicopters were ferrying tourists to magnificent Stradbroke Island. The tourist industry is really in full swing in south Queensland and both the governmental and recreational sectors are starting to wake up to the fact that a well-preserved environment is a valuable asset.

We might not have tempted a big jewie but I had enjoyed another day in paradise with David Green, and the good thing about fishing is that there is always the next expedition to look forward to. I might even try to catch a fantail leatherjacket off a game boat next time just to keep the skipper on his toes!

FACT BOX
Freeway bream at Southport

ROD: Light game rod for jewfish.
       Light whippy rod for bream.
REEL: Light game reel for jewfish.
       Light Shimano egg beater for bream.
LINE: 10kg for jewfish. 3kg for bream.
RIG: Running sinker.
BAIT: Live yellowtail for jewfish. Yellowtail strip for bream.
DANGEROUS FEATURES: Spines on bream.
TIME OF YEAR: Winter.
LOCATION: Southport Broadwater, south Queensland.

GET OUT THE TISSUES FOLKS. THAT MAN HOLDING THE WHOPPER ROCK HUT
CREEK WINTER RAINBOW IS GARRY BARMBY OF ANGLING ADVENTURES
WHO FLIES ALL OVER AUSTRALIA AND THE WORLD TESTING OUT THE
FISHING SPOTS SO HE CAN TELL US ABOUT THEM. IT'S A ROTTEN JOB...BUT I
GUESS SOMEONE HAS TO DO IT. *(Shane Mensforth)*

Winter rainbows

*SOMETIMES YOU JUST NEED TO GET AWAY AND RELAX
COMPLETELY, AND ON THIS TRIP I VISITED ONE
PLACE HIGH IN THE SNOWY MOUNTAINS WHERE YOU CAN
DO JUST THAT—AND CATCH FISH AS WELL!
PRIVATE WATERS CREATED SPECIALLY FOR ANGLERS HAVE
A PLACE ON THE AUSTRALIAN FISHING SCENE AND THEY
ARE NOW BEING WELL ACCEPTED.*

*I*f you create a fishery from scratch, stock it with fish and then add fine accommodation, it can become a haven for relaxation and a great place to enjoy a break. On this trip I visited Rock Hut Creek with a mate of mine called Garry Barmby. Garry runs a business called Angling Adventures so he gets the chance to fish all over the world. Garry tells everyone that he does all these trips so he can test the quality of the operations he books for, but I have a sneaking suspicion that he just loves fishing and any excuse is good enough! Being mixed up in the amateur fishing industry is a dirty job, but somebody just has to do it and we were both really hating the idea of spending a couple of days chasing big rainbow trout in the bracing air of a Monaro winter.

On our first session Garry decided to have a flick with his spinning rod and I rigged up my trusty fly gear. There was plenty of room for both of us to play our own games and I guess that is one good thing about having access to private water. There is plenty of space for everyone. The weather was about minus plenty, and Garry looked a bit like the abominable snowman in his long waders and his neoprene gloves. If you saw Garry walking along a city street in that clobber you would give him a dollar for a cup of soup, but up there in winter it was just what the doctor ordered. I suppose I looked like a refugee from the Russian front myself in all my gear and trusty beanie.

Garry struck first and a big buck rainbow thrashed on the surface as it took his little gold spoon. You just don't know what size fish is going to hit you in Rock Hut because they vary from about half a kilo to 4kg. This one was at least 2kg and it put up a great fight before Garry wrestled it to the shore. I think most people would have a heart attack if they regularly came into contact with fish as big as these Monaro monsters! Garry was using barbless hooks so releasing the fish was easy—just a matter of grabbing the trebles and giving them a twist with the pliers. It is a great sight to see a couple of kilos of hook-jawed buck rainbow swimming free, none the worse for a brush with a fishing fanatic.

If you catch a big one and you want to give it the chance to live a bit longer, there are a couple of things to remember. Whatever you do, don't squeeze the fish around the middle while you take the hook out. If a 15m tall giant grabbed you and squeezed you like an orange, you might walk away, but you wouldn't last long afterwards! Fish that have been squeezed hard die later when you can't see them. Try and leave the fish in the water as much as possible and be as gentle as you can while dehooking it.

After we watched Garry's fish swim away, I snuck along the reeds to where I had seen a healthy boil earlier in the day. My first cast landed gently right in close to the bank. Sure enough a big bow wave followed my fly on the retrieve. The old heart gave a bit of a flutter and I changed flies. I put on one of Rob Sloane's sunset flies and glided another cast into the hotspot. For a minute I thought I might have hooked Tony Lockett—the fish just went crazy, jumping and swirling all over the place. I was only using a 1kg tippet so the whole thing was a bit scary. About all I could do was to keep on using the rod as a shock absorber until the fish calmed down and I was in with a chance.

Eventually the big rainbow lay wallowing on the surface and I could cradle him and take out the fly. While I was holding him for the cameras I noticed another fly in his jaw. It turned out to be a small nymph that I had been using earlier in the day. That same fish had hit me really hard and broken the line by rolling in the weeds when I had hooked him earlier. I suppose that this just goes to show that the experience of being hooked and played couldn't be all that traumatic to a trout. Even the tiny hook imbedded in his mouth didn't deter the fish from having another go later in the day and crunching my sunset fly. Catching this fish was a real buzz for me! Big hook-jawed rainbows with crimson slashes down their flanks taking flies on light tackle at close quarters is just too good! Anyone want to swap jobs?

After these two fish Garry and I called it a day and headed for the lodge to have a couple of quiet ales and a feed. Sitting back and relaxing by an open fire and thinking about the fishing that we had just enjoyed made us very mellow. I'll drink a toast to the big rainbows of the Monaro any time!

FACT BOX

Winter rainbows

ROD: No 7 Sage Fly rod.
REEL: Hardy flyreel.
LINE: Weight forward No 7 flyline.
RIG: 2.7m tapered leader.
BAIT: Sunset fly.
DANGEROUS FEATURES: Freezing.
TIME OF YEAR: Winter.
LOCATION: Rock Hut Creek. Private water near Cooma, Snowy Mountains, New South Wales.

'GEE, MATE. A BIT OF THE OLD COLGATE WOULDN'T GO ASTRAY.'
HANDING OUT A REX HUNT SMACKEROO TO A SOUTH AUSSIE SWEEP.
(Shane Mensforth)

South Aussie sweep

SWEEP ARE ONLY A SMALL FISH BUT THEY GENERATE A LOT OF FUN AND THE PLACES THEY CALL HOME ARE OFTEN SPECTACULAR. I LOVE FISHING IN SOUTH AUSTRALIA AND THE CHANCE TO GIVE MY GOOD MATE SHANE MENSFORTH A BIT OF A HIDING WITH THE OLD PISCATORIAL WAND IS WELL WORTH TRAVELLING FOR ANY DAY. THE BIG V VERSUS THE CROWEATER IS ALWAYS A HARD FOUGHT TUSSLE WHETHER YOU ARE PLAYING FOOTY OR CATCHING SWEEP!

*T*he big thing with sweep is to fish right in under the white water. That is where they live, and if your bait is too far out, you just won't catch them. The sweep is perfectly adapted to his rocky turbulent environment. He is a chunky solid little fish and has to be fit to keep out of trouble when big waves crash onto the rocks and send huge volumes of water roaring all over the place. What sweep lack in size they make up for in fighting capability.

Sweep are specialists at eating small creatures that are dislodged from the rocks so they have to be able to manoeuvre accurately hard up against the rock ledges and around the kelp. When you hook one he generally knows just where to head in a hurry. The banded sweep is common in South Australia and it is a very handsome fish. The broad black bands against the silver scales stand out like neon signs and the effect is quite spectacular. The first 'double header' brought us two nice fish, but according to Shane they do grow much bigger. The banded sweep can reach lengths of around 45cm–and I can tell you right now that I wouldn't mind tangling with one of those! Still, two goals into the wind against the Croweaters isn't a bad start!

Shane says that these banded sweep have a big following in South Aussie because they fight hard and are very good to eat. Some people rate them up with snapper and whiting on a plate and that is a very big wrap. Targeting these fish from boats can be a bit hairy though because you have to put the boat in very close to the rocks to fish the white water. Unless you are a very experienced boat operator it would pay to fish from a charter boat. We were fishing from an 11.4m charter boat and our skipper Maris had his Coxswain and Master class five qualifications and he knew the area like the back of his hand. It is much easier to relax and enjoy your fishing if you have confidence in your boat and skipper. The last thing I want to see is a kid in a rubber ducky drowning himself to catch a sweep!

Actually, we weren't doing too badly on the sweep front, but at half time the Croweaters were gone for all money. I think Shane had filled me in too well on his sweep techniques! We were using a two hook rig baited with pipis, even though Shane insisted on calling them cockles. They are a strange lot, these Croweaters! The 'cockles' were baited up on chemically sharpened long shanked hooks and the trick was to cast into the white water and let the rig waft around until a sweep found it. If our rigs sank too quickly and ended up in the kelp we had serious problems with the kelp monsters. These denizens of the deep are parrot fish and they are the kings of the kelp. Anything (or probably anyone!) that finds its way into the kelp ends up in a parrot fish stomach! One of the ones I pulled up had both of my baits inside him. Fair dinkum, these fish swallow baits like Gary Ablett takes marks! With this type of fishing it pays to bring in your rig and re-cast it if you think it has reached the kelp zone. You have to have your bait under the white water, over the kelp, and hard up against the rocks–then you will catch sweep.

Shane told me that there is no bag or size limit on the species at all. There doesn't seem to be any shortage of them, so I guess that anglers aren't putting much of a dent in the population. Actually, I was very impressed by these little battlers and I wouldn't mind heading over again for another shot at them. Of course I would give Shane plenty of time to brush up on his tactics–I wouldn't want to win the next match too easily! Come to think of it, this sweep fishing could develop into a major competition between the states. Maybe not–if Shane let the rest of the Croweaters down next time in such an important event they might lynch him!

FACT BOX

South Aussie sweep

ROD: Light and whippy.
REEL: Light spinning reel.
LINE: 3kg.
RIG: Paternoster.
BAIT: Cockles.
DANGEROUS FEATURES: Being eaten alive by parrot fish.
TIME OF YEAR: Summer.
LOCATION: Cape Jervis, near Kangaroo Island, South Australia.

LEAVE ME OUT OF THOSE THUNDERSTORMS, THANK YOU VERY MUCH.
DAVID AND I RETREATED HOME AND DID A BIT OF MARINA FISHING
BETWEEN SHOWERS. *(Steve Starling)*

Thunderstorms on Pittwater

DAVID LOCKWOOD FROM MODERN BOATING TOOK US
TO A POPULAR NEW SOUTH WALES FISHING DESTINATION
FOR A SHOT AT SOME 'BREAD AND BUTTER' FISHING FOR
BREAM, WHITING, SNAPPER AND FLATHEAD. BUT THE OLD
WEATHER GODS JUST ABOUT BLASTED THE BEANIE OFF
THE BEARDED BURBLER AND DAVID AND I BOTH HAD TO
RETREAT JUST AS THE FISH WERE COMING ON. I AM KEEN
ON MY FISHING, BUT I'M THIN ENOUGH ON TOP WITHOUT
HAVING THE LAST FEW STRANDS INCINERATED IN A
LIGHTNING STORM!

The afternoon started off all right as we zipped over the calm surface of Pittwater in Dave's boat, and the scenery was surprisingly good for an area that is so populated. Low wooded hills drop down to a sheltered sleeky-calm series of arms; idyllic really, and it's no wonder that so many people love to fish and picnic in the area. Dave decided to fish a reefy spot off one of the points to give us the chance to catch a wide variety of fish, so after we pinpointed our location with the depth sounder, we dropped the anchor and started our preparations.

We rigged up with small egg beater style reels and light lines testing at about 3kg–this tackle is very versatile and it allowed us to confidently fish our small baits and light sinkers. When we started fishing, the action was slow for a while, so I decided to try and liven things up a bit with a bit of the old 'secret recipe' berley. My son Matthew and I have been working on a concoction that would attract Collingwood supporters to a Carlton pie night! Fair dinkum, the first night we tried it out, half the dogs in the Melbourne pound broke out and surrounded us on Altona Pier!

Seriously though, it is amazing how a bit of berley will stir up a dead spot and make it produce. Lets face it, there are millions of square metres of water out there and you want to attract fish to the few square metres that you are fishing in—berley is the best way to do it. After I had been throwing the magic potion around for a while, things started to happen and fish began to find our baits. First it was a tiny snapper, but even the appearance of such a baby showed that the smell of the berley was slowly seeping through the water and attracting interest. Now kids, come over and listen to Uncle Rex. Even if you haven't got any secret Rex Hunt berley, you can still throw bits of unwanted bait over the side to put a bit of the right smell in the water; and just about anything will do as long as it smells good to the fish. Prawn heads, discarded baits that have been chewed already, bait that is a bit old, or even a bit of Dad's sandwich are worth a go.

Things were definitely on the improve, and after the lean spell, we both started to catch fish on a regular basis. Dave was catching little cockney snapper hand over fist and I knocked off a lovely little black bream. None of these fish were monsters but they were all fun to catch and I thought that bigger things were on the way. As the afternoon faded into evening the weather really started to chill down and we needed all the clothes that we were wearing to keep warm. As the temperature dropped I put on my Glacier Gloves to keep my hands warm while I pulled in the beautifully marked juvenile snapper. Pretty fish—blue spots across the eyes, bright blue spots on the flanks, with crimson and silver shades playing across the flanks. The gloves that I was wearing are fantastic. They are made from wetsuit material and are designed so that the forefinger and thumb can be folded back to allow the angler to feel his line with his exposed fingers. If it gets too cold, you just fold the material over your fingers again and stay warm—great gadgets for fishermen and I really made good use of them on the Pittwater.

David and I were just starting to enjoy ourselves. We had the berley in the water, the fish on the bite, and the right gear to keep warm. Fishing is a funny game though, and something always seems to turn up to put a dampener on proceedings. In this case it was a southerly change complete with a raging lightning storm. There is no problem in fishing under tough conditions but when the boys upstairs start throwing lightning bolts around, it's time to head for the hotel and put on the old nose-bag. I took one look at the approaching storm and said to Dave, 'Mate, Sir Edmund Hillary, if he saw that, would jump off the top of the mountain.'

Now here is a lesson for the kids—if you are sitting in a boat on flat water with your rods sticking up in the air, you make a great target for any lightning bolt in the area. Lightning will hit the highest object around, so make sure that isn't you! Thunderstorms are bad news for fishermen so make like the old burbler and head for home if one brews up nearby.

You wouldn't believe it, but on the last cast before we left I pulled up a ripper sand whiting. This fish was as fat as mud and full of fight but I gave him the big kiss and let him swim to fight again another day. The water was dark and sloppy, the lightning was crashing around my ears and it was bloody freezing as Dave pulled the pick and we headed home.

FACT BOX
Thunderstorms on Pittwater

ROD: Light and whippy.
REEL: Light spinning reel.
LINE: 3kg.
RIG: Paternoster or running sinker.
BAIT: Fish strips and prawns.
DANGEROUS FEATURES: Spikes on fins of bream and snapper.
TIME OF YEAR: Winter.
LOCATION: Pittwater, north of Sydney.

GET A LOAD OF THAT GOB. NO WONDER THEY CALL SCHOOL TAILOR
'CHOPPERS'. JUST AS WELL WE WERE USING THE REX HUNT INVISIBLE HOOKS,
SO THERE WAS NO CHANCE OF THEM BREAKING ON THAT HARDWARE.

A red hot Queensland berley session with Peter Pakula

PETER PAKULA IS ONE OF AUSTRALIA'S TOP BLUE-WATER LURE MAKERS, BUT HE STILL LOVES HIS ESTUARY FISHING AND ON THIS SHOW HE DROPPED ME INTO ONE OF THE HOTTEST BITES YOU WOULD EVER WANT TO SEE. THE TAILOR AND BREAM WERE CHEWING THE BERLEY SO HARD THAT I RECKON THEY WOULD HAVE TAKEN THE OLD KITCHEN SINK IF YOU HAD TOSSED IT IN!

We were pumping the berley pot for all we were worth and a steady stream of fish flesh was clouding the water and drifting away with the tide. All fish love free tucker and we had a school of fish at the back of the boat that were ravenous. We were catching fish as fast as we could bait up and throw a line out the back and I was having a ball. Most of the fish were chopper tailor and they didn't get their name by accident. Even the word tailor has to do with the teeth of this species. One school of thought has it that the species was named because the fish had teeth as sharp as a tailor's scissors, while another naming theory is that they were called tailor because they have a habit of biting the tails off the smaller fish that they feed on. Whichever way you look at it these fish have serious teeth that are best avoided when you are removing hooks. If you see a bloke with fewer fingers than he should have, he probably works in a sawmill or he has been a bit careless pulling the hooks out of tailor!

In this session I was using some of the new Rex Hunt Signature hooks from Kmart. These hooks are bright red to act as an extra attraction to the fish and they have long shanks so that fish with teeth have a hard time trying to bite through the line. The hooks were doing a great job for us because they were quite acceptable to the bream as well as protecting our lines from the tailor. If we had just been targeting tailor we could have used sets of ganged hooks, or wire traces, but they would probably have put the more sensitive bream off their tucker. My Signature long shanked hooks did a great compromise job on both species and are always worth a try when you are fishing for toothy critters.

I pulled one of the bigger choppers in and (carefully!) unhooked him, then dropped him in the live bait tank in case we wanted to use him later as a bait for jewfish. As soon as I was back in the water another fish crunched the bait. This one felt a bit heavier and he offered me an opportunity to explain a little bit about the art of angling to our younger viewers.

When fighting a fish with light line we have to play a waiting game—if the fish pulls hard, we have to let him run a little bit or he will break the line. It is important that we don't pull at the same time that the fish does or we are in deep trouble. We let the fish tire himself out by pulling against a long shock-absorbing rod with plenty of bend, or by allowing him to pull line from the reel against a lightly set drag. The main rule of the game is that we don't start pulling until the fish stops pulling. This tactic forms the whole basis of sport fishing and it allows us to catch big fish on light line. It is a bit like a bungee jumping exercise—there has to be plenty of give in the system or, yibbida yibbida folks, the line will break!

The long rod that I was using was a great help as Peter and I hooked up fish one after another. There is a bit of a myth around that short rods are the only way to go when boat fishing, but that is a lot of twaddle. The long rod is a better shock absorber and it allows far better control of a fish during a hectic fight. There are all sorts of obstacles to counter when you are boat fishing and the long rod helps to keep the fish away from anchor ropes, motors, your mate's fish, and in my case a dirty great camera boat that was just about up my left nostril, if you don't mind!

There is another lesson to be learned from the action we had going on this show and that is to make the best of any fishing situation and maximise your results. Always work towards efficiency, not because you want to catch every fish in the sea, but because hot bites are normally short-lived happenings. Lots of things can interrupt hot sessions. Sharks or other predators can turn up and scatter the fish you have attracted to your berley—the weather can change and force you to leave, or the fish can simply decide to go off the bite. On this occasion we both took turns pumping the berley pot to ensure a constant supply of fish food and we both baited up and cast out absolutely as fast as possible so that we could have heaps of fun before something turned the fish off. Farmers might say, 'Make hay while the sun shines,' but Uncle Rex says, 'Get stuck in while the fish are on the bite!'

Beautiful Queensland weather, a super hot bite and the company of one of Australia's best fishermen made for a very satisfying television segment and I really enjoyed the opportunity to pass a few tips on to the youngsters. That's what it is all about, having fun and priming up our next generation of anglers so they can enjoy their fishing in the future.

FACT BOX

A red hot Queensland berley session with Peter Pakula

ROD: Light spin.
REEL: Egg beater spinning reels.
LINE: 3kg.
BAIT: Cut fish strips.
DANGEROUS FEATURES: Teeth on tailor. Spines on the fins of the bream.
TIME OF YEAR: Winter.

THAT'S MAGNIFICENT HINCHINBROOK ISLAND IN THE BACKGROUND WITH
MOUNT BURNET IN THE DISTANCE. IT'S HARD TO GET ANY BETTER FISHING
THAN IN THE MANGROVE LINED CHANNELS AROUND THE ISLAND.
(Keith Graham)

Magnificent Hinchinbrook - home of the barramundi and the croc

The Hinchinbrook Channel near Ingham in North Queensland is absolutely breathtaking. It is a 300 square kilometre maze of saltwater creeks, mangrove flats and small mangrove islands. John Simmonds from North Australian Sport Fishing knows the area like the back of his hand and on this show he guided us through the tangled mangrove channels and put us on to a variety of interesting fish.

It is hard to believe just how spectacular this Hinchinbrook area is—there is water everywhere you look, and on windless mornings the surface shimmers with magic reflections off the mist-shrouded hills that rise straight out of the sea. The old burbler has been all over the place in an effort to bring you folks some interesting fishing but this place is just so visually fantastic that it takes the breath away. Right from the water's edge, the mangroves support life—their roots are covered with oysters and they shelter crabs and schools of small fish.

As you look up from the water the trees become thicker along the steep slopes that bracket the wetlands, and the whole effect is like a Steven Spielberg set. There are even some real dinosaurs to look at in the form of large crocodiles that lie on the mud banks and slide into the water when the boat gets a little too close.

AND THIS IS WHAT HINCHINBROOK IS FAMOUS THE WORLD OVER FOR...
BARRAMUNDI...AND THERE'S PLENTY OF 'EM. FOLKS, YOU HAVEN'T LIVED UNTIL
YOU'VE BATTLED A BARRA. *(Keith Graham)*

While the crocs are at the top end of the food chain, this fantastic estuarine system is home to a wide variety of life. There are dugongs, hundreds of species of fish, crabs, birds, mammals and other exotic forms of marine creatures. The place just seethes with life. I am always on about the environment, but a lot of people don't know how important mangroves are to our fish stocks, even down south. A huge percentage of our commercial fin fishery along the east coast of Australia is dependent on species that use the mangroves as nursery areas at some stage in their life cycles. Snapper are a prime example. Juvenile snapper hide and feed among the mangroves in our estuaries until they are old enough to head for the ocean to become targets for recreational and professional fishermen. That is why it is tremendously important to save big areas of mangroves such as we have at Hinchinbrook.

John drifted us along a likely bank and we both started lobbing lures close to the cover with our baitcast outfits. One of my favourite lures up north is the small Nilsmaster Spearhead and that is what I tied to the end of my line. I really enjoy this type of fishing–the rhythm of casting the finely tuned Shimano Chronarch reel and the expectation that my lure could be monstered at any time is a buzz. We came to a sheer rock face that looked a sure bet to hold a fish and I got that fishy feeling as the old Nilsy lobbed in hard to the bank. A couple of winds and then, bang, the rod-tip was pulled down hard and I was into something that wanted to get back under the bank in a big way. After fighting well early the fish lost its sting rapidly and we soon had 'Old Catfish Joe' next to the boat. These northern catfish take lures intended for other species on a regular basis and unhooking them can be dangerous.

The cattie wasn't really what we were after but it did offer me an opportunity to show some of the danger points that catfish have. There are three very bad spines on a catfish that you have to avoid at all costs because they are venomous and can really knock you around. One of the spines is located at the leading edge of the dorsal fin (that's the fin on top) and the other two bad ones are on the pectoral fins at the side of the head. The spines are very strong and if you stand on a catfish, even with running shoes on, the spike can still penetrate your flesh. These fish are best dehooked with the aid of strong pliers. In fact most experienced northern sports fishers have a pair of pliers hanging on their belts just so that they can take the hooks from anything that they catch.

After the catfish we drifted down a channel with thick mangroves lining the bank and threw our lures deep into the hidden recesses that we hoped would hide fish. My lure landed right back in a shaded slot in the greenery and sure enough I had a bump on my lure as I started the retrieve. I stopped the lure and then pulled it along in small jerks to make it look wounded. The tactic worked well and the fish came back and nailed the lure. It was no world-beater but when he came to the boat we could see he was a very colourful cod. Cod are actually quite aggressive predators and grow to enormous proportions in the estuaries. The fact that this fish had a grab at the lure without connecting is also fairly typical of northern estuary dwellers. If you are up that way and feel a tap on your lure, don't give it away, keep the lure moving in an erratic way as though it has been crippled and you might get crunched. If nothing happens, bung the lure straight back where you had the hit and the fish might still be interested. Never be too keen to leave a spot where you have had some action.

The little cod I had caught had just about swallowed the whole lure to demonstrate how big a mouthful they will attempt to eat. It isn't unusual to catch cod that are about the same size as the lure you are using. Cod remind me a bit of my boy Matthew, they will try and eat anything!

When John Simmonds brings his clients to Hinchinbrook they usually catch plenty of different species including barra and blue salmon; it really is a good place for a smorgasbord. John mentioned we were approaching a bit of a hotspot with a rock bar and some snags near good mangrove cover. When we noticed schools of bait-fish flipping around the area as well, we both started to feel lucky. Fish aren't too different from us when you think about it—in human terms this spot was like a block of flats with a pizza parlour outside it! A roof over your head and plenty of tucker on hand—the fish just had to be here.

Sure enough, there was a great commotion amongst the bait and John had his lure monstered by a giant trevally. Unfortunately he didn't stay connected, but the strike certainly got both of us in the mood–and the baitfish were still agitated. I threw my little fluoro Nilsy into the middle of the bait school and something whopped it hard. It wasn't a big fish but it fought hard and the bounce in my line made me think that it could have been a trevally. Trevally are usually easy to pick because they turn on their sides when they feel the hook and their steady pulsing lets the angler know what he has on the end of his line. Yep, this one was a small trevally and although he was nothing to write home about, he pulled like hell and gave me a tough fight.

The action was warming up as we approached the turn of the tide, and that seems to be the case just about anywhere that you fish. It pays to know at what time the tide changes on any particular day and then you can make sure that you are fishing in a good location at the right time. The classic mistake is to fish hard all morning and then to have lunch or some form of break just as the fish are coming on. The schools of herring were becoming more active and something was certainly bothering them. John landed his lure close to the rocks and something solid took it and locked the rod up. The fish made a couple of strong lunges and then jumped–just what we wanted, a healthy barramundi. There is no doubt about it, barra are special, and when John finally had the fish beaten beside the boat we could see all his subtle colours–purples, bronzes and the whole thing flashing with silver. Magic Johnny, just magic. As I was removing the hook we had time to admire the prominent eyes that make the barra an ideal night stalker and gave some thought to the streamlined mouth that can open up like a bucket when tucker time comes around. It doesn't matter how many barra you catch, you just don't get sick of them.

This was a great spot and the barra was probably hunting here because, for him, the conditions were ideal. Dirty water from upstream was meeting clear seawater and stirring up nutrients that feed the bait schools. Barra know a good ambush spot when they find one and quickly take up residence.

John's fish topped the day off for us, and it had been a wonderful session. It is a real privilege to fish in this unspoiled wilderness area of Hinchinbrook and I hope that I get the chance to come back with John some other time to sample more of its beauty and its fish.

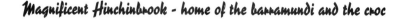

FACT BOX

Magnificent Hinchinbrook

ROD: Baitcaster.

REEL: Shimano Chronarch.

LINE: 8kg.

RIG: Double and 15kg trace.

LURES: Wobbling lures and deep diving lures.

DANGEROUS FEATURES: Cutting spike on barra gill plate. Sharp scutes on trevally tail. Catfish spines.

TIME OF YEAR: Summer.

LOCATION: Hinchinbrook Channel.

'I AM NOT AN ELEPHANT. I AM A FISH.' YOU COULD HAVE FOOLED ME!
LOOKING MORE LIKE A CROSS BETWEEN JIMMY 'SNOZZLE' DURANTE
AND THE ELEPHANT MAN, THE ELEPHANT FISH PUTS UP A GOOD FIGHT AND
IS GREAT EATING. *(Geoff Wilson)*

The elephant fish of Westernport

'MUD, FLOOD OR BLOOD—YOU HAVE TO GET OUT HERE
TODAY.' MY SON MATTHEW WAS DEAD KEEN TO GET
MYSELF AND THE CREW OUT OF BED AND ONTO
WESTERNPORT TO SHOW HOW TO KNOCK OVER A FEW
ELEPHANT FISH, AND HE WASN'T BEATING ABOUT THE
BUSH WHEN HE WAS BURNING MY EAR ON THE PHONE.
TALK ABOUT WEIRD CREATURES—THESE FISH LOOK LIKE A
CROSS BETWEEN 'SNOZZLE' DURANTE AND THE
ELEPHANT MAN AND TO TELL THE TRUTH, EVEN WITHOUT
THE URGING, I WAS LOOKING FORWARD TO A DAY FISHING
FOR THEM ON WESTERNPORT WITH MY BEST MATE.

Even the way elephant fish swim is different, they sort of undulate their fins when they are moving slowly, but are capable of bursts of speed that can surprise you and break your line if you aren't careful. I guess that they are a surprising fish in general. They are not a well known species, even though they are found close to Melbourne, so I thought that they would make an ideal subject for a segment on 'Rex Hunt's Fishing Australia'. My son runs a charter operation and fishes for whiting and snapper, but at times schools of elephant fish turn up in his territory and his customers always love fishing for them. We intended to fish out from the Westernport Marina and were hoping to find a concentration of fish so we could guarantee plenty of action for the television show. Matthew had been taking quite a few fish over the preceding few days on his

ONLY A MOTHER COULD LOVE IT. THE ELEPHANT FISH THAT IS, NOT
GEOFF WILSON, WHO'S HOLDING IT. AND I CAN TELL YOU THAT THERE WAS
NO CHANCE OF 'LONGUS SNORKUS' GETTING THE OLD
REX HUNT SMACKEROO TREATMENT. *(courtesy Geoff Wilson)*

charter operation, and he reckoned that the tides and the weather would be perfect if we could make the time to get there. No problem–I'm a busy man these days with football and fishing, but when my best mate says there are fish to be caught, I'm only too keen to drag the crew out of bed and head for the action.

It is about an hour and a half run from Melbourne to Westernport, but we made it into the boats in fair time and Matthew and myself were setting up the gear early to hit the peak time as the tide really started to run. These fish love pilchards and we rigged them up snapper style–that is, with a Mustad 4190 hook run-in under the gill cover and out just before the eye. To complete the rig we wrapped the line around the body of the pilchard a few times and then did two half hitches around the tail. This bait survives the attention of small pickers but the exposed hook is just about a sure bet to snare anything big that takes the bait. The gear we were using was the same stuff that Matthew uses on his whiting charters–a Garry Marsh Southern Gold rod, a Shimano AX 3000 reel and a line of around 3kg breaking strain. This is light gear, but it seems to handle the fish well enough and I reckon we hook more of them on the sneaky gear than we would on heavier tackle.

We lowered our rigs into the tide and waited. Conditions were perfect and the bay was one huge mirror that seemed to bend up at the edges and blend into the haze. Waiting, waiting, waiting–even though fish had been coming in over the preceding days, there was no guarantee that they would show up for the cameras, so all of us were hungry for the first sign of action. Eventually it came, and Matthew's rod gave a couple of thumps and then buckled over as a good fish pulled line from the little Shimano egg beater. I was stoked that the young bloke had hooked up, and he was very confident that we were finally in contact with old 'longus snorkus'. He was right.

The first elephant fish gave Matthew some stick on the light line, but eventually it came to the surface and the relentless pull of the whippy rod soaked the fight right out of it. These fish are truly beautiful as they plane along just under the surface–their brilliant silver bodies and fins glisten and shine against the pattern of glowing black bars, and their fins ripple like flags as they come to the net. I have seen a lot of fish, but these things are something else. The most common response from someone seeing an elephant fish for the first time is: 'Would you take a look at *that*!!'

On the show, I got Mattie to explain a bit about the elephant fish, because they really aren't all that well known to the angling public. In autumn they come into the lower reaches of Westernport to spawn, and anglers are starting to wake up and target them at that time of year. Blowing the whistle on their breeding habits on national television will put more pressure on the species, so I hope you don't rush out and fill ten sacks up with fillets, and then dump them on the mother-in-law! We don't know how sensitive these fish are to harvesting yet, so it might be a good idea to go easy on them while they are testing out the old wedding gear in the bay. If you do manage to put one in the boat, watch out for the spike on the first dorsal fin—it is a real 'doozey'. Fair dinkum—I reckon that spike would puncture the tyre on a tank! These creatures are actually fish although they have no backbones and their skin is scale-free. This is why they are mistakenly called sharks by some people. Unfortunately for the old elephant fish, he has beautiful boneless fillets that taste terrific. I guess you can't help bad luck!

As the net went under our first fish, the pressure of the day was off and I really started to enjoy myself. Even so, further fish were hard to come by. For the next couple of hours absolutely nothing happened. Now I keep saying on the show that perseverance is the greatest asset you can have in fishing—you just have to keep trying when things are tough—and in this case the waiting game finally paid off. Not one, but two fish hit at once. This is dream stuff when you are making a television show and it finished off a great session on a high note as we landed both fish. We got great shots of the pectoral fins on the elephant fish undulating wildly as the fish came to the boat, and I guess that I will always remember these living jewels as something special after that day. Fishing with my own son also gave me a lot of satisfaction and if you have a son of your own, make the time to take him fishing—you can't beat being on the water with your own flesh and blood.

FACT BOX
The elephant fish of Westernport

ROD: Light and whippy.

REEL: Light egg beater.

LINE: 2.7kg or less.

RIG: Mustad 4190 2\0 Hook as lightly
weighted as conditions allow.

BAIT: West Australian pilchards.

DANGEROUS FEATURES: Spike
on first dorsal.

TIME OF YEAR: Autumn.

LOCATION: Westernport.

ROB BROWN RELEASES A NICE FLATHEAD IN THE 'FLATHEAD CLASSIC',
ORGANISED BY MY MATE DAVID GREEN. *(David Green)*

*T*he purists would faint, but trolled up trout provide lots of fun. Just ask the cunning old Fox.

*T*erry Shephard with a 1.5kg brown trout caught in the Eildon Dam. Trouble was that all of that hair kept blowing in front of the fish, threatening to ruin the picture. It's a long, long time since I've had that problem folks.

*J*immy Allen just loves those Bermagui bluefin and takes them on in just about any weather conditions. *(Glen Booth)*

Peter Pakula with a whopper lizard taken in Greenie's Flathead Classic.
(David Green)

*W*ith David Lockwood after a successful night on the hairtail in Sydney.
(Steve Starling)

*O*ne of my favourite pastimes–signing autographs for the kids.
(Paul B. Kidd)

*T*he Rex Hunt Invisible Hooks I mentioned in the Peter Pakula berley story. You just can't beat 'em folks. (*Paul B. Kidd*)

*P*eter Pakula returns a bream to the water after it copped the legendary Rex Hunt smackeroo.

*A*nd when the Bermagui bluefin aren't on the bite, Jim Allen doesn't mind
the odd bit of yellowfin tuna fishing with sensational results.
(courtesy Jim Allen)

'**N**ow folks, before I give you a guided tour of my new game fishing boat, I'd like to point out...' On location in Sydney. *(Paul B. Kidd)*

On Sydney Harbour waiting for a bite. On days like this, a fish is a bonus. *(Paul B. Kidd)*

*N*ow why didn't they have able bodied seamen (ladies, folk, persons) when I was eligible to join the navy. Signing autographs on location in Sydney. *(Paul B. Kidd)*

*M*ore Southport Breakwater jewies. Remind me to give Greenie a ring and get up there and catch a couple. *(David Green)*

Flathead trolling with David Green

FLATHEAD ARE COMMON TARGETS FOR MANY ESTUARY FISHERS BUT TROLLING FOR THEM HAS ONLY RECENTLY BECOME A WIDELY ACCEPTED FISHING OPTION. DAVID GREEN ORGANISES THE FLATHEAD CLASSIC, WHICH IS THE ONLY EVENT OF ITS KIND IN AUSTRALIA, AND HE SHARED SOME OF THE TRICKS OF THE TROLLING TRADE WITH US ON A QUEENSLAND FLATHEAD SESSION. I LOVE FISHING WITH GREENIE BECAUSE HE IS AN EASYGOING BLOKE AND HE REALLY KNOWS HIS ONIONS.

We were fishing just off Crab Island north of Surfers Paradise and Greenie was working hard to find us a fish. A lot of people think that trolling is a hit and miss situation, but that just isn't true. For the flathead segment on my show, Greenie and I were dragging our lures around to try and put them right in front of hungry fish. Flathead love to lie just where the shallow water slopes off into deep water so that they can ambush small fish and prawns as they drift past. Greenie was looking intently at the sounder so we could run the boat along the edge of a likely drop-off in about 2.4m of water. The lures we were using ran from around 1.8m to 2.4m deep so we knew we were presenting the fish with something they could see and attack without rising too far from the bottom.

Now kids, listen to the bearded burbler for a minute. In all fishing, you need to find out what sort of territory your target fish likes to live in, and then you give him a look at something he just can't resist. In this case we picked the right terrain, we used lures that ran at the right depth, and because the old flattie likes to chase down his tucker, we trolled them past at a fair speed. When you get a chance to take Dad flathead trolling, make sure he looks at the sounder and selects a lure that runs at a depth that will take it close to the bottom.

Always keep an eye on your rod-tip when you are trolling, because if your lure is working properly the tip of your rod will vibrate with a familiar movement. If this vibration changes, you know that your lure has fouled with weed or picked up some other piece of junk. Attention to detail is what makes one fisherman more successful than another–if you don't notice that your rod-tip has lost its action, you can waste a lot of fishing time.

We were using a variety of lures such as Stumpjumpers, Rapalas and Nilsmasters but they all have similar characteristics. Flathead like a lure with plenty of action and all these brands of lure put their heads down and their bums up, and they all wriggle like hell! These active lures work well even if you misjudge your depth a bit and they dig their bibs into the sand. Something that actively swims down and digs up sand just has to be alive as far as a flathead is concerned.

We didn't have to troll far before a little winter flattie nailed my orange Stumpjumper. It was only a small fish but it proved the point that the fish were keen to cooperate if we got the system right. Even small flathead have nasty spikes on each side of the head and also on top in the dorsal fin. If you do catch one it pays to flip the fish over and grab him in the vee of the gills. That way he can't drive any of his spikes into you. Although this first fish was legal size we put him back to grow again another day. Greenie explained to me that all the fish taken in the Flathead Classic competition are released, including the whoppers–what a great thing to see some of the best fishos in the country travelling a zillion miles to fish and then leaving everything they catch to breed or provide fun for other anglers. Just give them the old Rex Hunt kiss and off they go. There is no doubt that is the way I like to see competitions run.

Greenie copped another flathead, but again, it was only a small fish. Fishing isn't always about catching giants, that's for sure, and if you can take the family out and catch a few fish on the troll, just puttering along in the sunshine, then I reckon that's just fine. How about these dusky flathead though, they really are a great predator when you consider that these small fish we have been catching are knocking off quite large lures running at a fair pace.

Yeah, bread and butter fishing, that's what it is all about–not everyone can go out chasing marlin, but all it takes to troll for flathead is a little tinnie, a couple of inexpensive outfits and a bit of nous. If you get the chance this weekend why not grab the 'billy lids' and make like Greenie and the burbler–we had a ball catching flatties on the troll and I reckon you would too.

FACT BOX

Flathead trolling with David Green

ROD: Light baitcaster.
REEL: Small baitcaster.
LINE: 3kg to 4kg.
LURES: Small deep-diving lures.
DANGEROUS FEATURES: Spikes at side of head
and on dorsal.
TIME OF YEAR: Big fish in summer, smaller fish in winter.
LOCATION: Crab Island, Queensland.

'Rex Hunt's Fishing Adventures' tackle expert, Jim Allen, loves catching whopper bluefin and accepts that the best time to do it is in a howling gale.

Southern bluefin in a hurricane!

IF THE WAVES ON YOUR TELEVISION SET LOOKED BIG DURING THIS SHOW, THEY LOOKED BLOODY WELL ENORMOUS TO ME IN REAL LIFE WHEN GRAHAM BAKER DRAGGED ME OUT OVER THE SHELF TO CATCH MIGHTY BLUEFIN TUNA OFF BERMAGUI. FAIR DINKUM, I RECKON WE WERE CLOSER TO NEW ZEALAND THAN WE WERE TO AUSTRALIA! I MUST HAVE SEEN WORSE WEATHER, I JUST CAN'T REMEMBER WHERE.

Even Graham Baker remarked that the conditions were 'not too favourable'—I wouldn't like to be out with him on his idea of a bad day! Anyway the conditions were ideal for bluefin as they are renowned for coming to the top in rough weather. Jim Allen, the crew and I were trolling a pattern of lures behind the boat about 55km from shore, where the professional fishermen set their long-lines, and we were confident that sooner or later we would get lucky. I've always said that the harder you work at fishing, the luckier you get—and in this case Graham Baker and the crew of *Ultimate* had all the fishing gear, from the big Tiagra game reels to the finely tuned lures, in top shape.

The fishing gear on a state-of-the-art game boat such as *Ultimate* probably looks very confusing to young anglers or those who prefer simple shore-fishing methods, but Graham took some time on this show to explain how the outriggers are only poles to spread the lines out so a couple of extra lures can be trolled. The outriggers have clips on them and the line passes from the rods on the outside of the boat,

THE ROUGHER IT GETS, THE MORE THEY LIKE IT—THE SOUTHERN BLUEFIN
TUNA THAT IS. NOT THE OLD BEARDED BURBLER'S IDEAL CONDITIONS, BUT IF
THAT'S WHAT IT TAKES TO BRING OUR VIEWERS THE BEST FISHING FOOTAGE,
THEN I'LL LEARN TO PUT UP WITH IT. *(Paul B. Kidd)*

through the clips and then is trailed behind the boat. When a fish strikes the outrigger lure, the clip releases and line is retrieved in the normal manner on the reel.

They go to all this trouble because a pattern of lures looks far more attractive to a school of fish than one or two individual ones. The lures used out here are also very different from something that you might cast into the Yarra River for a trout–they are about 30cm long and 4cm around the plastic head. The rest of the lure is a multi-coloured skirt of vinyl plastic that swims and vibrates as the lure is dragged behind the boat at seven or eight knots. These lures look very spectacular in action and they leave a distinct trail of bubbles behind them. Big fish follow the bubble trail and then hit the lure–or at least that is the theory! The rods that are in the middle holders on the back of the boat are called flatlines because the line comes straight off and goes directly to the lure splashing along behind the boat. When the wind is blowing across the boat like Jimmy Allen snores (and I can tell you that *is* fierce) the lines can get blown together and tangled, so we pull the line down and tie it to the reel handle with a rubber band. This puts it a lot lower and the wind doesn't affect it as much. When a fish strikes, the band breaks and the fish can be played normally.

Graham runs bigger lures from the outrigger poles and smaller straight running lures from the flatlines to cope with the rougher water in the wake of the boat. The lures are run on about the sixth wave spreading back from the boat, which means that the lure sits about 30m from the rod-tip. There is also a dirty great 'dentist's' chair in the middle of *Ultimate's* cockpit. I thought that Graham might have pulled a few teeth in the off season, but the chair is designed to support fishermen while they fight heavy fish. You might have also noticed that the rods are clipped to a great thick rope like my mate Guiseppe Rizotto used to use for a handline on the Altona pier. This is a safety line in case some idiot drops the lot over the side! Each outfit is worth about four grand, so I would say that the safety line is a top idea.

Well, there we were, four lines out, and four lures creaming down the monster waves and leaving bubble trails across the water that

Blind Freddy could have found. The wind was having fun blowing the tops off the waves and I was starting to wonder if I was ever going to see dry land again.

There is something about the wail of the ratchet on a big game reel that just hits you in the guts—no more thoughts about the weather. I grabbed the rod and staggered to the chair with it. Whatever I was connected to felt like a submarine, but I had a fair idea that it was what we had come all the way out here to catch—a big bluefin tuna. This was a really tough fight and I was working like a one armed paper hanger trying to renovate the Taj Mahal—I even had to wake Jimmy Allen from a serious snoring session so he could position the chair for me and make the fight a bit easier. Fair dinkum, I felt as though I had played a whole game of footy including the time on, but the fish was nearly at the boat. Now, this is a tip for the kids—when you are nearing the end of a hard struggle with a fish, take it easy. Make sure your drag isn't too tight, because your fish is going to play up at the last minute for sure, and when you have him on a short line there is no stretch in the line to get you out of trouble. Most big fish that escape, do it in the last minutes of the fight.

When we use heavy line, the last few feet are doubled over with a special knot called a plait, and then a very heavy trace is tied on so the deckie can grab the line close to the fish and pull him up to be gaffed or released. I was just about knackered by the end of the fight and I was starting to think that this might be my last fish ever, when Rick, our deckie, took the trace and struggled the fish to the side of the boat. There he was at last, gleaming vibrant blue and mirror silver, with beautiful golden fins, a massive tuna—'*maaagnificent*'. The boys pulled him onto the deck, he got the old Rex Hunt smackeroo, and then it was back into the drink with him. These fish are heavy and it was a big effort to lift this one over the side so he could carry on with his life.

I have to hand it to Graham—he is the best game skipper I have seen, and after taking us out in those conditions probably the maddest!

We reset the lines and then things went quiet for a while. At least the fish went quiet; the wind really started to whistle, and it was blowing about 40 knots from the north. You wouldn't believe it though, as soon as I went below for a doze, we got knocked off again by another bluefin. Out onto the deck and back to work. Jimmy Allen reckoned that the crook weather was turning the fish on and that the same thing happens on the Tasmanian bluefin grounds. My philosophy is that the bad weather follows Jimmy Allen around. If you want bad weather, just take Jim along and batten down the hatches!

These tuna just don't know when to quit, and this one was no exception–he put his head down and made Uncle Rex tough it out. Eventually Rick took the trace and manhandled the fish almost over the transom. The hook tore free and the fish took off none the worse for his encounter with the old bearded burbler. That's one I didn't get to kiss.

Well, I guess that is what it is all about–game fishing is a team effort. Graham driving the boat through productive areas, Rick setting up all the gear, and the big fella doing all the hard work on the rod. This was one of our toughest assignments but we came up with the goods and it was satisfying to show you folks a bit about big waves and bluefin tuna.

FACT BOX
Southern bluefin in a hurricane!

ROD: 15-24kg gamerod, roller runners.
REEL: Tiagra game reel.
LINE: 15-24kg monofilament.
RIG: Double, heavy mono trace, Mustad stainless 10\0 hook.
LURES: Large pusher lures.
DANGEROUS FEATURES: Powerful tail that can
break human limbs.
TIME OF YEAR: Autumn.
LOCATION: Bermagui, wide over the continental shelf.

WHEN IT COMES TO CATCHING FISH, ANDREW JARMAN AND CHRIS
MCDERMOTT MAKE A COUPLE OF GREAT FOOTY PLAYERS. SO DON'T WORRY
SOUTH AUSTRALIA, YOU'VE GOT NO CHANCE OF LOSING EITHER OF THEM TO A
CAREER IN FISHING. *(Shane Mensforth)*

Footy stars, but fishing bums!

ANDREW JARMAN AND CHRIS MCDERMOTT ARE TWO OF
THE BEST FOOTBALLERS TO COME OUT OF SOUTH
AUSTRALIA, BUT THEY WOULD PROBABLY BE GOOD
CONTENDERS FOR THE WORST FISHING PAIR TO EVER
CAST A FISHING ROD AWARD! I LOVE FISHING WITH 'JARS'
BECAUSE WE ALWAYS HAVE A BALL AND I AM
CONTINUALLY AMAZED AT HOW BRILLIANT HE IS AT
SCARING EVERY FISH FOR A HUNDRED MILES.
FAIR DINKUM, IF YOU COULD CATCH A FISH WITH EITHER
OF THESE GUYS ON THE BOAT YOU WOULD BE A GENIUS.

We had blasted out from Adelaide in a fast boat to have a crack at the whiting that were supposed to be there. With the two Crows on board, of course the whiting were not in evidence. I can't understand why Andrew doesn't catch more fish though. He is an absolutely brilliant footballer, and he obviously uses the same hairdresser that I do! Ah, well—I've never seen anyone enjoy catching nothing more than Andrew does.

We were just starting to relax and enjoy ourselves when the unthinkable happened—Chris got a bite. Yes, the old rod-tip quivered and a fish was on. When this mighty denizen of the deep appeared before our eyes, the whole team nearly fell out of the boat laughing. As far as we could guess, we had battled and landed a species that is a rare rod and reel capture—yes folks, it was the mighty West Australian pilchard! I'm Rex Hunt and you're not, and I have travelled a zillion miles by boat and plane to catch a baitfish!

THEY MAY BE GREAT ON THE FOOTY FIELD FOLKS, BUT OUT IN THE DEEP BLUE
YONDER ALL ANDREW JARMAN AND CHRIS MCDERMOTT COULD ACCOUNT
FOR WAS TIDDLERS LIKE THIS TINY MACKEREL.
I'M GLAD YOU THOUGHT IT WAS FUNNY FELLAS. THE OLD BURBLER THOUGHT
IT WAS. . .YIBBIDA YIBBIDA. . .PATHETIC. *(Shane Mensforth)*

Remember that you saw it on 'Rex Hunt's Fishing Australia' first.

By this stage things were looking grim on the fish front so I started to give Andrew a bit of a ribbing. I had to ask the question—'In three shows with me, how many fish have you landed, Jars?' And the answer, 'One'. I rest my case as to how bad this guy is as a fish jinx.

Chris was having a purple patch, however. He outdid himself by hooking a leatherjacket that he eventually landed after an epic struggle. The old Elvis Presley came in clacking its teeth and raising and lowering its dorsal spike. These are a really pretty fish with blue spots and undulating fan-like fins that allow them to manoeuvre around the reefs. The teeth on these fish are like bolt cutters and you need long-shanked hooks so that they don't bite through the line when they are on the way up to the boat. After I pulled the long-shanked hook out of the fish and gave him the mandatory kiss, he swam away back into the depths. Andrew even managed to kiss the Elvis, but I don't think his heart was in it!

We might not have set the world on fire as far as the fish went, but it was a real pleasure to share some time with a couple of legends, and to give you people a chance to see that there is another side to the superstars of the AFL.

THE FOX WITH A TERRIFIC TROLLED-UP TASSIE TROUT. SOME FOLKS THINK
THAT TROLLING IS THE LAZY WAY TO CATCH TROUT BUT WITHOUT A GUIDE LIKE
FOXY, IT CAN BE VERY BORING AND UNPRODUCTIVE.

Trolling Tassie trout with Foxy

LAKE SORELL IS A BEAUTIFUL PLACE TO BE, EVEN IF THE SKIES ARE GREY AND THE WIND IS WHISTLING AROUND YOUR EARS. THERE IS NO-ONE I WOULD RATHER HAVE WITH ME ON A TROUT TROLLING EXPEDITION THAN JOHN FOX, AND ON THIS SHOW HE SPILLED THE BEANS ON SOME CUNNING TACTICS FOR MY FAVOURITE FRESHWATER SPECIES—THE BROWN TROUT.

There is no doubt that Tasmania saves up her meanest weather for the old bearded burbler, so every time I head for the Apple Isle I make sure that the beanie and raincoat are the first things into the suitcase. On this trip I was glad that I had prepared well, because the wind hadn't bothered to stop anywhere between the South Pole and my backbone! Talk about lazy—it just went straight through me!

We launched the boat into Lake Sorell with plenty of confidence because it is usually the top lake in the State on a catch per angler basis. It is quite a picturesque place to fish, as the shore is heavily timbered and the eucalypts run right to the water in places. On the day that we decided to fish however, the conditions were bleak. The water had a grey gunmetal appearance, and the whitecaps chased each other towards the far shore. Foxy assured me that these conditions were just what we needed to bring a few fish on the bite so I snugged the beanie down a bit tighter and set my rod in the holder.

Now trout trolling is seen by some folks as an easy way to catch

NOT A WHOPPER BUT CERTAINLY CAUGHT IN BETTER CIRCUMSTANCES THAN
WANDERING AROUND IN THE MIDDLE OF FREEZING LAKE SORELL.
AS YOU CAN SEE FOLKS, I STILL NEEDED PLENTY OF RUGGING UP.

fish. This is a long way from the truth and I see trolling as being similar to making money. The harder you work, the luckier you get, whether you are trying to make a living, or trying to put your lure past a hungry fish. There are a lot of factors to get right before you start catching fish on the troll.

For a start, the speed has to be just right to make your lure swim properly. Experience has shown Foxy the best speed to travel at, and the way to consistently maintain that speed is to watch your rod-tip vibrating. If you go too fast, the tip goes crazy, too slow, and the tip loses all activity. In practice it is easy to keep an eye on the tip and keep the boat at a productive speed.

John was watching his tip like a hawk and we hadn't gone far when I saw his rod buckle over and heard his drag squealing in protest as a decent fish grabbed his lure. This was more like it but the fish fell off. The funny thing was that Foxy had just begun to tell me to expect a hit when the action started. Was he pulling my leg, or did he really know just when to expect a hit?

Foxy was serious all right, and he went on to tell us one of the tricks to trolling successfully in Lake Sorell. Trout like to feed where there is a concentration of food, and one of the best places to find food in any trout lake is along sunken weed-beds. Underwater banks and drop-offs usually have good weed growth and also attract small fish and crustaceans. The trick is to pick out such locations with your depth sounder and then to troll your lure right over them. It also helps to know how deep various lures travel so you can pick one that will run just above the bank that you have picked up on your sounder.

I've got a little Lowrance portable sounder on my own boat and it is a great help when I am trolling. Being portable, I can take it off the boat and leave it in my room when I am not fishing. That way it can't be knocked off!

On a fair-sized boat like John's, it pays to have all mod cons such as depth finders, radios and even a GPS if you can afford one. The sounder can find the productive areas, the GPS can take you back to them, and you can always ask your fellow trollers how they are going on your radio.

Anyway, we backtracked over the shallow ground and this time Foxy's rod thumped hard as a good fish hit his lure. In this game you've got all the time in the world, and John carefully worked his fish to the boat and I gently placed the net under it. Just take your time and it is almost too easy.

The lure that worked well for John was a black and silver McGrath minnow that catches fish just about anywhere. The colour scheme has plenty of contrast and the lure gets deep enough to pull fish off the weed-beds. It doesn't really look like any food source in the lake but it wriggles well and fishes at the right depth.

After we landed Foxy's fish the weather started to look like the inside of a cow–black and wet! Fair dinkum, a bloke needs two beanies to fish in Tassie! We persevered though and just as we passed a visible weed-bed my little Stumpjumper got nailed in a big way. My Shimano baitcaster reel went into reverse at a rate of knots as a decent brown dived for the weeds. This fish was a battler but the smooth drag and whippy little rod worked overtime and soon had him under control. When you are tackling any trout on lures, remember that they are often lightly hooked and any sudden jerking from your end can tear a hook loose. This time the fish made it to the boat and it was a beauty! Sorell fish have lovely markings and this one was no exception. A dark green back, silver sides, and bright red spots–magic.

Most of the time we use a net to land trout that we catch from a boat, but there are other ways to go about it if you don't happen to have one with you. I decided to use this fish to demonstrate the comfort lift to viewers. This technique depends on sliding your hand underneath the balance point of a fish and very gently raising your hand until the fish is lying clear of the water. Most of the time this operation can be completed and the fish stays completely immobile. If you are attempting the comfort lift, always be prepared to drop the fish if it kicks. If a fish suddenly comes to life and you wrestle with it, you can find yourself with a handful of treble hooks! And then it's, yibbida yibbida, time for the doctor folks!

On this occasion the fish did kick, and then disappeared back into the depths! The look on John's face was priceless because he was already licking his lips in anticipation of a fine fish dinner. I wasn't too concerned because I have a bit of a soft spot for the old brown trout and didn't mind seeing this one head for home. After that the weather really cracked up and we headed for home ourselves. It had been a great day in the Tasmanian high country chasing the elusive trout and a good opportunity to show you folks at home that there is more to trolling than meets the eye.

THERE'S NOTHING THAT THE OLD BEARDED BURBLER LOVES MORE
THAN CATCHING GIANT SNAPPER LIKE THIS PAIR (CAUGHT AT WHYALLA, SA).
AND THERE'S NO SHORTAGE OF THEIR SMALLER COUSINS AT
FABULOUS BERMAGUI. *(Shane Mensforth)*

Bermagui reef fishing with Jim Allen

FISHING ISN'T ONLY ABOUT THE BIGGEST OR THE BEST. SOMETIMES WE NEED TO JUST RELAX AND BOB AROUND THE OCEAN IN THE SUN FOR A WHILE. THE FOUR MILE REEF OFF BERMAGUI IS THE PERFECT LOCATION FOR A BIT OF 'HAPPY HOOKING' AND MOST OF THE TIME YOU CAN EVEN KNOCK OFF A FEED OF SNAPPER FOR THE FAMILY. WHEN JIMMY ALLEN MENTIONED THAT THE REDDIES WERE HAVING A GO ON THE REEF, IT TOOK ME ABOUT THREE MINUTES TO RING THE CREW, PACK THE RODS AND HEAD FOR THE ACTION!

There is something special about Bermagui in the morning. It is usually calm and tranquil inside the port, and the bright morning light hits the white hulls of the fishing boats and scatters across the water and the rocks. Pelicans sit in a row along the sandbank and watch as boats go over the bar. Back in the thirties, Zane Grey captured some of this magic in his books and now Rex Hunt is bringing some of it to people through the medium of television. The great thing about Bermagui is that it really hasn't changed much—the atmosphere is still there. I love the anticipation of being on the water early and as I walked down the wharf with my fishing mate Jim Allen, I was really looking forward to a pleasant day doing what I like best.

Graham Baker is a top skipper and he runs one of the smartest game boats in the port, so he is my man in Bermagui. Jim and I clambered on board *Ultimate* and Graham soon had us rounding the pine-studded headland and heading for the famous Four Mile Reef. Earlier in the year, around autumn, this reef is the site for some frantic yellowfin tuna fishing, and as we made our way out, Jim regaled us with tall tales and true of his exploits with the big game tackle. Jim gets fairly fired up about the big game stuff, and I had a tough job to settle him down and persuade him to drop a line for one of my favourite fish. Snapper!

Snapper are one of the fish that first captured my imagination, and you might say that I cut my teeth on them in Port Phillip Bay. The old snapper is a truly brilliant fish—his scales gleam red and the blue spots on his side glow like little lights. The snapper fights well, takes a bait hard and tastes terrific. Wherever you find them, the old bearded burbler wants to catch them, and that is a fact.

Graham wasted no time putting us on the spot and once the anchor was down we rigged our gear. We were using rods around 2m long and overhead reels that were capable of holding about 200m of 10kg line. Some of my readers might find it strange that we were using rod and reel combinations rather than the more traditional handlines for our reef fishing. This modern fishing tackle actually has plenty of advantages over the old handline system. For a start, it is much neater, as your line is stored on the reel, rather than all over the deck. Another major plus for the fancy gear is that it is much more versatile than a handline. When we are fishing deep reefs we just don't know what is going to turn up next. Large fish are always on the cards and it is better to tackle them with plenty of line and a good drag system rather than burn your hands and run out of line with a handcaster.

Our terminal tackle was simple enough, with a light sinker and two hooks on droppers. On this particular day the current was not running all that hard, so the light sinkers did a good job of presenting the baits. On days when there is a strong current running, you just have to go up in sinker size. Bait size is not absolutely critical when you are fishing reefs for bottom-dwelling fish, but if you cut a strip of fish that is about as big as your little finger, you will be in the ball-park.

Once we had the gear rigged and baited, it was just a matter of dropping the baits over the side and watching them slide down through the clear water. The waters off Bermagui are so clear you can watch the baits go down till they are just tiny shining specks.

The fish were on the job early and Jim and I got stuck into them in a big way. Sometimes they even came up two at a time! Occasionally when you are fishing deep and you pull the fish up in a hurry, their air bladders blow up as the pressure decreases near the surface. When this happens the small fish have trouble reaching the bottom again once you have released them. It is possible to spike the swim bladder so that the fish can return to the bottom, but the procedure isn't foolproof.

This time I had no trouble with my double-header of little snapper. First one and then the other darted away smartly when I kissed them and slid them into the water. These small fish are the ones we will be chasing in a few years, so it pays to release them as carefully as possible.

This bottom fishing caper is just what the doctor ordered for frazzled nerves. If there are a few of you on a boat, you can enjoy a bit of light-hearted banter and still catch fish. While we were fishing, one of the local bottom bouncing boats was in action not far away. Keith Appleby and his boat, the *Tarpin*, are institutions around Bermagui. Both have been around forever and both have plenty of character. As we watched, the group on *Tarpin* were having a ball. Jimmy probably hit it on the head when he said that you don't have to pay $600 a day to catch marlin and yellowfin to enjoy yourself. Some folks are more than happy to go to Bermagui with the family to spend a few days relaxing and catching a variety of reef fish. When you think about it, the top fisherpeople of tomorrow are out there now as kids learning their trade on the breakwalls and jetties, and on 'happy hooking' boats like *Tarpin*. It is a great way to start kids ocean fishing because they are taken out by licensed skippers who know the waters well, and they are looked after.

Now kids, listen to Uncle Rex for a minute. If Mum or Dad does organise you a trip out on a charter boat there are a few things that will help you to have a good day. If you haven't done much ocean fishing it will pay to take some form of motion sickness medication. Plenty of top fishermen suffer from seasickness but with the aid of a pill now and then, they are fine. The chemist will have a few choices and you might have to try a couple of different pills before you find one that works for you. Even if you do get a bit crook, it is worth persevering, because most folks find that seasickness affects them less as they do more trips. Just getting up early in the morning and being excited by the prospect of the fishing often upsets tummies. Make sure that you take plenty to eat as well because if you keep a little something inside you, that often helps to make you feel better. A bottle of soft drink is also a must as the bubbles and sugar seem to soothe the stomach.

Anyway, the crew of the *Tarpin* must have taken all the right precautions because they looked to be having a ball. We were doing pretty well ourselves and I was struggling to crank up what seemed

WHILE OFFSHORE BERMAGUI PROVIDES SENSATIONAL FISHING, ONSHORE HAS ITS HIGHLIGHTS AS WELL. IN THE TRUE TRADITION OF ZANE GREY, THE HORSESHOE BAY HOTEL IS A SUPERB REMINDER OF A BYGONE GOLDEN ERA.

(Steve Starling)

to be a better fish. This one was a ripper, about 3lb on the old scale and in absolutely prime condition. The only way I was going to kiss this one was goodnight, because he was destined to go in the old Rex Hunt nosebag for dinner. Jim was cranking away like crazy as well but when his fish hit the surface it looked about as appetising as the three eyed one on 'The Simpsons'! Fair dinkum, this thing had more spikes than a golf shoe! I took time out to have some fun with Jim but while I was giving him a hard time he snuck down another bait and an even bigger snapper than mine ate it.

After that, even Jim had to admit that there is more to Bermagui than just marlin and yellowfin. Jim might have won the honours for the best looking snapper but he also had a stranglehold on the prize for the daggiest hat ever seen on television! I reckon he shops at the same store that Worsel Gummidge uses, and Worsel is a fake scarecrow on kids' television!

There is no doubt about it, reef fishing off Bermagui is a lot of fun and I think that we should remember that is what fishing is all about. We had certainly had a ball making this segment and I was looking forward to a sizzling snapper fillet for dinner.

FACT BOX

Bermagui reef fishing with Jim Allen

ROD: 3m, solid butt, whippy tip.
REEL: Overhead. Capacity 200m of line.
LINE: 10kg.
RIG: Mustad 4200 on two snoods.
BAIT: Fish fillet cut.
DANGEROUS FEATURES: Spines on snapper fins, crushing teeth.
TIME OF YEAR: Winter.
LOCATION: Four Mile Reef, Bermagui.

A *MAAAGNIFICENT* MARY RIVER BARRAMUNDI
CAUGHT ON A LURE WITH BARBLESS HOOKS WHICH MAKES IT A LOT EASIER TO
TAG AND RELEASE THEM WITHOUT KEEPING THEM OUT OF THE WATER TOO
LONG OR UNNECESSARILY HURTING THEM. *(Alex Julius)*

Mighty Mary River
barra

THE MARY RIVER DRAINS A HUGE FLOOD-PLAIN AREA THAT IS ALIVE WITH BIRDS, ANIMALS AND BIG CROCS. THESE DAYS IT ALSO BOASTS A FINE HEAD OF BARRAMUNDI. PHIL HALL WAS MY GUIDE ON THIS EXPEDITION AND HE TOLD US HOW THE NORTHERN TERRITORY FISHERIES DEPARTMENT TOOK A LONG HARD LOOK AT THE DECLINING BARRA FISHERY IN THE AREA AND THEN DECIDED TO MANAGE THE FISHERY AS A PURELY RECREATIONAL ONE. THEIR DECISION CAUSED AN OUTCRY AT THE TIME BUT IT HAS PAID OFF IN A BIG WAY.

I t is probably worth having a look at how the Northern Territory Fisheries Department resurrected what was once a great barra fishery. Barra have been under huge pressure for a long time in the north of Australia from both amateur and professional fishermen. The truth of the matter is that they just couldn't take the pressure and the species was on its knees in many of the popular areas. In their wisdom, the department decided that the future lay in a recreational fishery rather than a traditional commercial one, and they planned accordingly. For a time they banned the capture of fish altogether so that the survivors would have a chance to spawn unmolested. They radically thinned out the ranks of legal commercial netters, and then they brought in strict bag limits for anglers. The plan worked like a charm and now tourism is booming and the dollars that recreational fishing brings into the Territory dwarf what used to be the meat value of the pro catch.

THE MARY RIVER'S FAMOUS BARRAGE AT SHADY CAMP WHICH SEPARATES
THE TIDAL WATER FLOW FROM THE UPSTREAM FRESH WATER OF THIS PROLIFIC
BARRAMUNDI RIVER. BUT DON'T FALL IN AS THE GIANT CROCS RATE THIS
HIGHLY ON THEIR FAVOURITE RESTAURANTS LIST. *(Alex Julius)*

The sooner some of our other fisheries managers recognise the value of recreational angling and manage their waters accordingly, the better. It has been estimated that every barra caught by a tourist is worth $5,000 to the Northern Territory!

Now you know why fabulous Phil Hall was so confident of finding a few barra when we launched our boat into the rushing waters of the Mary River. Straight after the wet, all the water that has been deep over the plains in the summer runs off down the river and into the sea. It brings with it all sorts of interesting things for barra to eat–frogs, small rainbow fish, insect larvae and just about any small creature that washes down. Barra take up positions where any drain or rivulet runs into a main stream so they can take advantage of the free supply of tucker that comes their way.

We were fishing the Mary at the famous barrage, built to keep the sea from encroaching on the wetlands, and apart from the fishing, the scenery was just fantastic. The aquatic vegetation is so lush with many different shades of green–reeds, grass, trees and water-weeds. Even the fish take on the hues of their surroundings and they are a magnificent bronze with green reflections around the head and mouth. I keep saying that this is a dirty job, and someone has to do it, but I'll let you in on a little secret–being able to visit locations such as this one keeps the old bearded burbler on cloud nine!

Many of our viewers head north for a shot at barra, so I asked our man on the spot to talk about a few of his favourite lures. Phil shares my respect for the Nilsmaster Spearhead and that is what I tied to the end of my line as a starter. This lure has a tight wriggle that barra seem to love and it is a bite-sized morsel that appeals to a wide range of fish. Because the Mary River system is a designated recreational fishery only, we used single hooks on our lures to make releasing fish easier after a limit of two was taken. Other popular lures for barra include the Stumpjumper range with the detachable coloured bib and the larger Nilsmasters that are more likely to appeal to bigger fish. Since I fished the Mary, I have come across another lure called the Tilsan Barra that is made in Australia and is as tough as nails. This lure is fast becoming one of my favourites because you can't break it and barra love to eat it!

This wet had been bigger than normal and the water movement was difficult to comprehend. Everywhere there were rushing streams of water flooding down towards the ocean. In this huge volume of water, we found it difficult to locate fish. They had to be there, but where? I reckon that my winding hand must have clocked up a few kilometres but we still hadn't had any joy. If you want to do well at anything though, you have to keep going when times are tough. It doesn't matter if you are having a lean run at playing footy, or if you have been crook, or if you are having a bad time at school—you just have to persevere. Life can be awfully hard at times, but you will never get anywhere if you give up.

I kept flogging the little Spearhead into every likely looking spot and, sure enough, eventually my lure came to a dead halt and my line bucked off the spool of the little Chronarch. When fish are playing hard to get, you have to handle the ones that do strike carefully. I had the best possible gear to do the job this time, so I was confident that I would land the fish. My Loomis rod was made from high quality graphite and that meant continuous pressure could be applied through the fish's lunges and jumps. The Shimano Chronarch reel has a state-of-the-art drag system that protects the line from sudden jolts, and I was completely confident of its performance. This is what I try to get across to our young fishers, attention to detail pays off.

The little single hook stayed firmly in the fish's mouth and after a few more desperate lunges, Phil slid the net under 4kg of prime barramundi. Phil thought that this fish had come straight down from the swamps because of its coloration and condition. The fish was as fat as mud and very fit.

You can see that the single hook rule works well because my hook just slid out of the fish as soon as Phil gave it a yank with his pliers. Removing trebles is often more difficult and can stress fish to the point where they don't recover. A thumb grip on the fish was all it took to pick it up and then it was just a case of kiss it goodbye and ease it over the side so that some other lucky angler could perhaps catch it in the future. There is no doubt about it, barra are special. They have big googly eyes that are very effective by day and by night, and a hell of a big gob to eat anything that happens along. I love my whiting, snapper, and trout, but on my last day on the planet, if I can kiss one of these magnificent barramundi and watch it swim away, I will go into the furnace a happy man!

Fishing the Mary River with Phil Hall is a great experience and just goes to show that fisheries management can make a huge difference. If the direction comes from the top and a fishery is managed as a recreational one, there are major benefits to be gained. Recreational fisheries generate huge revenue, and only a small proportion of a fish population needs to be taken to allow this to happen. I take my hat off to the Northern Territory Fisheries Department for their foresight and I can tell you that Rex Hunt will be right behind any southern fisheries department that decides to take a similar initiative.

FACT BOX

Mighty Mary River barra

ROD: Light Loomis Graphite Baitcaster.
REEL: Shimano Chronarch Baitcaster.
LINE: 4kg mono.
RIG: Small double and 15kg Mono Trace.
LURES: Nilsmaster Spearhead Lure.
DANGEROUS FEATURES: Spines on fins, cutting spike on gill cover.
TIME OF YEAR: Autumn.
LOCATION: Mary River near Darwin.

OUR 'REX HUNT'S FISHING ADVENTURES' MAN AT CAPE JERVIS, MARIS ZALUPS, WITH A 1KG PLUS 'ELBOW SLAPPER' WHITING. I'M GLAD TO KNOW THAT THEY REALLY EXIST BECAUSE ALL HE COULD FIND FOR THE OLD BURBLER WAS JUST ABOUT ANYTHING BUT. *(Shane Mensforth)*

Jackets, wrasse and BPs

Folks, one of the nicest things about my job is going to interesting places and meeting interesting people. Maris Zalups is our man at Cape Jervis and we were fishing at a place called Tunkalilla near Kangaroo Island. Maris told me that Tunkalilla meant place of bad smells and not surprisingly, it is just near Backstairs Passage! Thank you very much Maris! To make matters even worse the local whiting had done the bolt and we had been catching Maori wrasse that are nicknamed BPs in most parts of the country. If you don't know what BP stands for, well that's bad luck, because I run a family show and this segment was already starting to smell bad!

Actually, I had a lot of fun with Maris and he is one of the characters that make fishing such a delightful sport. Maris keeps his sturdy charter boat on a trailer and launches it with a tractor. I think we made quite a sight driving down the street with Maris perched on his tractor and the big fella riding shotgun on back of the boat–'wagons ho'o'. The Southern Ocean is wide open in this part of the world and even on relatively quiet days such as we had, there is always a 'joggle' to keep you on your toes. There is plenty of fresh air and the views are certainly expansive, but somebody must have told the fish that we were coming, because they would not cooperate at all. We did manage some leatherjackets and a few reef fish, but the majority of our catch seemed to be BPs. Apparently these fish are well accepted as table fish down here, but I was a bit dubious about trying them after the reputation they have elsewhere.

If you plan enough trips, sooner or later you have to hit an area when nothing much is happening but Maris told me that the fishing is generally much better. We still managed to catch a lovely horseshoe leatherjacket. The colours on these fish are fabulous—they have a brilliant purple skin with bright yellow blotches on the sides. They would have to be one of the best eating fish you could find anywhere in the world. This one was also one of the luckiest fish in the world, because I felt sorry for him and all he had to wear was the Rex Hunt kiss, instead of Maris Zalups's frying pan!

Maris loves taking people out on his charter boat and he gets a big kick out of helping beginners catch a feed of fish. We might not have set the world on fire on our shot at Tunkalilla, but fishing with Maris was entertaining and very relaxing. If you caught bags of fish every time it just wouldn't be the same and we always tell it as it happened, win, lose or draw. When you watch 'Rex Hunt's Fishing Australia' you see the real thing.

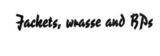

FACT BOX

Jackets, wrasse and BPs

ROD: Shimano, light and whippy.

REEL: Light egg beater style threadline.

LINE: 4kg.

RIG: Paternoster with two droppers.

BAIT: Squid and fish flesh.

DANGEROUS FEATURES: Spike on leatherjackets, teeth on wrasse.

TIME OF YEAR: Autumn.

LOCATION: Cape Jervis, an hour and a half from Adelaide.

GEORGE THE MOGGY CAN'T BELIEVE HIS LUCK AS JACKIE GREEN WAVES A
BREAM UNDER HIS NOSE. BUT NOT TONIGHT GEORGIE BOY! THAT BREAM
COPPED THE REX HUNT SMOOCH AND WAS SENT HOME. *(David Green)*

Kids, fish and berley

ADD ONE FAMILY TO ONE JETTY, MIX IN A BIT OF BERLEY, STIR WITH SOME ADVICE FROM DAVID GREEN AND REX HUNT, AND YOU HAVE THE PERFECT RECIPE FOR FISHIN' FUN, JUNIOR STYLE. LOTS OF MUMS AND DADS WANT TO TAKE THE KIDS FISHING, SO WE THOUGHT IT WOULD BE A GOOD IDEA TO RUN THROUGH SOME OF THE HANDY HINTS THAT CAN MAKE A FISHING TRIP FOR THE KIDS MORE INTERESTING AND PRODUCTIVE.

I just love catching fish from piers and jetties, I did plenty of it when I was a kid and just because I have been around a while and the old beard has a bit of white in it doesn't mean that the thrill of catching a fish has diminished. Watching kids catch fish is even more fun than catching them for yourself anyway.

I met Gemma, Michael and Jackie on Peter Pakula's jetty and we set up for some serious fishing. Well, George the cat must have thought it was serious anyway, because he kept looking expectantly into the water to see if anyone had hooked any cat dinner. Kids usually have short attention spans so it is important to do all you can to ensure that they get plenty of action. David had provided us with a bucket of mulched up bread for berley and as soon as we spread some of it around, fish started to appear under the jetty and the kids started to get some bites.

This berley trick is the mainstay of fishing with youngsters. Kids often have lower expectations than we do as far as the size of the quarry is concerned, but they really appreciate quick action. In Australia, if you throw enough bread into the water in just about any waterway–small fish of some sort are going to turn up. It doesn't matter much to kids whether the fish they catch are garfish,

KIDS, PIERS AND FISHING JUST HAS TO BE THE BEST COMBINATION EVER INVENTED. GEMMA GREEN WITH A BREAM THAT ROSE TO THE BERLEY, WAS CAUGHT AND LET GO. *(David Green)*

bream, mullet, slimy mackerel or yellowtail, as long as they are hungry and they keep on coming!

Once you have the berley trick under control, make sure the kids have plenty of small hooks. This is important because a small hook will catch tiddlers all day but will also take hold on any larger fish that snoop round the berley. If you give the kids big hooks, they become discouraged quickly when they keep losing baits without hooking up.

If you can find a safe jetty such as the one we were fishing from, or you can let the kids fish from a boat, all you need to start off with is a simple handline. It is easy for the kids to understand exactly what is happening when they are fishing with gear as basic as this and they get a good grounding in the sport from the bottom up. Two of David's kids were using handlines and Jackie was using a rod because she was a little older and more experienced. If you are starting your youngster off with a rod and he or she is right handed, leave the reel handle set up on the left hand side of the reel. It is much more efficient to fight the fish with your dominant hand and to reel with your other hand. This might seem clumsy at first but it pays off in the long run. Kids are amazingly adaptable and they pick up good habits in a flash if you show them the correct technique.

They say that you shouldn't appear with kids or animals and that is probably not far from the truth! Young Michael took the opportunity on national television to pay out on the big fella–he reckoned that the last time we fished, I waited for him to go to sleep and then ate his sandwich! Believe me folks, the old burbler would never steal a kid's sandwich–er, at least I don't think he would.

We were having a good time but I think that George the cat was the only one with real faith, he watched every move with interest and really got excited when Jackie hooked a fish and battled it to the surface. This wasn't a bad sort of bream, and it gave Jackie a fair workout as it dived for the piles of the pier. Young talent prevailed in the end and the fish eventually made the perilous journey from the water to the deck. The fish had swallowed the hook, but David (well-prepared as usual) nipped off the hook with a small pair of clippers. This hook swallowing act on the part of the fish is an occupational hazard when you are fishing with kids because they haven't yet developed the feel to know when to set the hook.

The small hooks that we use when kid fishing are also easy for fish to swallow. When a fish is deep hooked and you want to release him, his best possible chance of survival is assured if you just cut the line as close as possible to his mouth. Unless the hook is a stainless one, it has every chance of rusting away. Jackie was brave enough to do a Rex Hunt on the fish and she planted a good old smackeroo on the top of its head before it splashed back into the drink. There is no doubt about it, fishing with kids is great, and it is fantastic to see so many youngsters these days letting unwanted fish swim free to be caught again another day or to breed and ensure our fishing for the future. Fishing with the Green family in Queensland (and George the cat) was a lot of fun and I hope that you will pick up a few of these family tips and take your own family out for a fish.

FACT BOX

Kids, fish and berley

ROD: Handlines and light spinning rod.

REEL: Egg beater.

LINE: 3kg.

BAIT: Prawns.

DANGEROUS FEATURES: Spikes on bream.

TIME OF YEAR: Winter.

LOCATION: South Queensland.

MY MATE JUNIE DALTON FISHING THE MOYNE RIVER FOR BREAM. AND THE
LITTLE LADY CAN OUTFISH THE BLOKES ANYTIME. ONCE JUNIE HOOKS UP—IT'S
YIBBIDA YIBBIDA, THAT'S ALL FOLKS.

Junie on the Moyne

*LADY ANGLERS ARE ON THE INCREASE, AND WHY NOT?
JUNIE DALTON JUST LOVES TO FISH THE MOYNE RIVER AT
PORT FAIRY AND SHE IS A GENUINE 'GUN' ANGLER.
JUNIE REPRESENTS VICTORIA EVERY COUPLE OF YEARS AT
THE AUSTRALIAN CHAMPIONSHIPS SO SHE DEFINITELY
KNOWS WHICH END OF THE ROD TO HOLD.
I WOULD LOVE TO SEE MORE WOMEN TAKING UP THE
SPORT BECAUSE SEX IS NO BARRIER TO FISHING FUN.
LET'S TAKE A LOOK AT THE LOVELY MOYNE RIVER AND
SOME OF THE FISH JUNIE CATCHES THERE.*

I have had a soft spot for the Moyne River for a long time so I was really looking forward to fishing with Junie. The weather gods smiled on me as well because the morning dawned clear as a bell and completely windless. When you get a good day in this part of the world it is likely to be a cracker. The whole scene looked like something out of a postcard, it was just so neat and ordered and precise. The jetties are well maintained and the white mooring posts were all reflected in the still harbour water. There seems to be a sense of relaxation about this place, the yachts and fishing boats come and go but they don't seem to be in a big hurry. The town is backed by huge pines in a neat row, and well-kept lawns run right down to the rock groyne where Junie was waiting for me.

I asked Junie for a bit of a forecast as to what we might expect to catch on national television and I got a bit more than I bargained for! I can see why this girl is good, folks, because she has plenty of confidence. With an answer that included 'couta, trevally, sea mullet, bream, zebra fish and luderick, she had the old bearded burbler just about stumped! It might have been easier if I had asked what we weren't going to catch!

We were using sandworm on a running sinker rig and I had no sooner rigged up and cast in when the old rod-tip started to twitch like my manager's nose does when he smells money. Next minute the fish was on and he bolted along the rock wall like a bullock. I had to yell for our cameraman Harry to follow me while I tried to control the fish. At the bottom of the groyne there are plenty of loose rocks that a fish can burrow into and a long rod is a big help in preventing bust-offs. In the old days there was no rock wall here and the Moyne just flowed out into a delta in Bass Strait. To the local fishing fleet a substantial wall was constructed and eventually the underwater part of this structure was covered by a lush weed growth. This weed, and the loose rubble, combined to make a prolific feeding area for many different types of fish.

Eventually my custom-built Garry Marsh special subdued the fish that turned out to be a top class bream. These Moyne River bream are real studs—solid right through, with heavy shoulders. I rather think that Junie fancied this fish on a plate rather than back in the water—but this one was all set for a big sloppy kiss and an attempt on the Olympic diving record. Yes folks, it was a double back flip, with pike, that resulted in a perfect entry.

We had just finished releasing this fish when the biggest conger eel you have ever seen calmly swam along the surface right next to the wall. This thing had to be about 14kg in weight! It just stooged along and quietly wandered away. The Moyne River is full of surprises!

I gave Junie a try with my long rod and she hooked another good bream straight away. It is good to watch an accomplished angler in action and Junie gave a great demonstration of how to fight and land a fish in difficult terrain. In places like the Moyne there is no substitute for that long rod—it just takes the kicks and lunges in its stride and, with it, you can hold the fish out and away from any obstacles. They don't call Garry Marsh the rod god for

Junie on the Moyne

nothing–he really knows how to select the right blank and make the most of its capabilities.

One of the best parts of my job as I fish my way around Australia is to seek out and find some of our interesting fishing characters. Junie Dalton was a delight to fish with and I hope that any ladies out there with a bit of a yen to go fishing take a leaf out of her book and get into it. There are already plenty of women fishing and I would like to see more of them giving it a shot.

FACT BOX

Junie on the Moyne

ROD: Long and whippy.
REEL: Shimano baitrunner, egg beater style.
LINE: 3kg.
RIG: Running sinker.
BAIT: Sandworm.

DANGEROUS FEATURES: Spikes on fins of bream.
TIME OF YEAR: Winter.

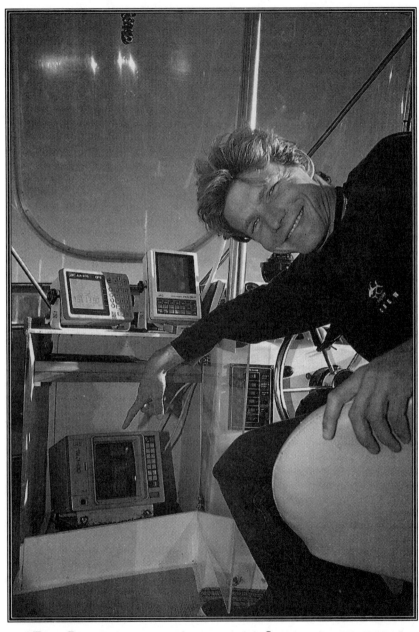

TONY DAVIS WITH THE ELECTRONICS ON HIS SYDNEY CHARTER BOAT, *FISHFINDER*. I'M GLAD HE KNOWS HOW TO USE THEM FOLKS, 'COS I'M JUST ALONG TO CATCH 'EM, NOT FIND 'EM. *(Paul B. Kidd)*

Charter boat gadgets with Tony Davis

MANY PEOPLE FISH ON CHARTER BOATS, BUT THE ELECTRONICS USED BY SUCCESSFUL SKIPPERS USUALLY REMAIN A MYSTERY. I CLIMBED ON TO THE POPULAR FISHFINDER IN SYDNEY HARBOUR FOR A QUICK LOOK AT THE THINGS THAT MAKE THE BOAT TICK. IT WAS ACTUALLY VERY INTERESTING AND THERE IS MUCH MORE TO BEING A SUCCESSFUL SKIPPER THAN LADY LUCK.

According to Tony Davis operating a charter boat is no different to any other aspect of fishing. You have to have the right equipment to get the job done or you just don't succeed.

The first gadget that caught my eye was the GPS–most of you will have heard the initials often enough but you may not know the exact function of the device. GPS is a Global Positioning System that uses a number of satellites to tell you exactly where you are on the surface of the planet. This is a very useful thing to know when out on the ocean fishing. You can find a good spot and then punch an 'event' marker on your unit. This means that you can track your way back to exactly the same spot any time you want to. When you are a charter skipper folks don't want to be mucked about, they want to catch fish, and with a GPS you don't waste time–it is just a case of heading directly for the hotspots. These things are also marvellous navigation aids because you can find exactly where you are even in a fog or at night. The sets can also give you other useful information such as how fast you are going and how long it will take you to reach your destination. Computerised plotters use charts that come on discs and it is possible now to cover the whole planet with a cupboard full of tiny pieces of plastic. This beats the hell out of having a room full of paper charts!

There are some misconceptions around as to how accurate GPS really is. The system is an American one designed and used by the military for pinpoint navigation and bombing. We know the system is capable of pinpoint accuracy, but the US military doesn't want everybody lobbing accurately placed bombs back on them, so they scramble the signals somewhat for ordinary users. Even with the scramblers operating, the system is fairly accurate—just don't try to drive your boat through a narrow rocky channel straight off the plotter—Uncle Sam could be playing tricks on you at the time!

The good ship *Fishfinder* also carries a radar unit. Even though a GPS does some of the jobs that a radar used to be essential for, it has not and will not ever completely replace radar. A GPS will tell you where you are all right but it will not tell you if you are about to be run over by a freighter! Radar is also great for picking up large flocks of birds before they can be seen with the naked eye.

Depth sounders are now standard equipment on most amateur boats, and charter boats usually have a fairly fancy colour version of the same thing. The sounder tells you how deep the water is and it can also find schools of bait and larger fish. Colour sounders are a great aid to gamefishing charter operators because they can differentiate between normal bait schools and the dense, bunched up ones that are being hassled by large predators.

If you are out on a bottom fishing charter you can be assured that the skipper will have his eyes glued to the sounder screen. The sounder can tell an experienced operator the type of bottom he is fishing over. It might be mud, sand, rock or weed but the skipper will be able to tell from the sounder display. At times it is even possible to tell which species of fish are down there. The particular colour of the targets and often the configuration of the schools gives the operator his clues as to which species is present.

We could see from our quick look around on *Fishfinder* that charter skippers like Tony Davis are working hard to ensure that their customers have a good time and catch fish. If you go out on a trip and you can't see the skipper you will have some idea of how he is spending his time. Nothing happens by accident in fishing—if you have been catching fish somebody has been working all the angles.

COME ON IN A BIT CLOSER FOLKS AND I'LL TELL YOU HOW TO CATCH
MORE FISH. IN THE NEXT SECTION YOU'LL FIND SOME OF THE OLD
BEARDED BURBLER'S *SECRET* FISHING RIGS, BEAUTIFULLY DRAWN BY
AUSTRALIA'S LEADING FISHING ILLUSTRATOR AND 'REX HUNT'S FISHING
ADVENTURES' REGULAR, GEOFF WILSON. WHEN YOU HOOK UP ON ONE OF
THESE, IT SHOULD BE YIBBIDA, YIBBIDA. . .THAT'S ALL FOLKS. *(Paul B. Kidd)*

Rex's favourite rigs

WHEN I AM TRAVELLING THE COUNTRY IN SEARCH OF DIFFERENT FISHING EXPERIENCES I TRY TO STICK TO A FEW BASIC RIGS. THE PATERNOSTER RIG, THE RUNNING SINKER RIG, AND THE SIMPLE GAME FISHING RIG USING A DOUBLE AND A HEAVIER MONO TRACE ARE ALL I NEED TO COVER MOST FISHING SITUATIONS.

When I am fishing northern blue water I use the common single strand wire rig. When I am chasing barra and other estuary species on lures I use a 24kg monofilament trace tied to the lure with a loop knot to allow the lure to wobble well. If you follow the diagrams closely on the next few pages, you will know how to construct these rigs and your fishing success should increase.

Once you understand the basic construction it is possible to vary the rigs slightly to cover different fishing situations. For example, the Paternoster rig can be varied by tying longer or shorter snoods off the main line. The sinker weight can be made heavier or lighter to suit the conditions and the size and gauge of the hooks can be selected to suit the target species and the bait to be used. The running sinker rig can be varied by changing the length and the breaking strain of the trace and the size of the hook. The weight of the running sinker can also be selected to match the conditions.

These rigs have been tried and tested over the years and they are the ones that have produced the goods for me on national television. I hope they work well for you!

BERLEY FLOAT RIG FOR GARFISH

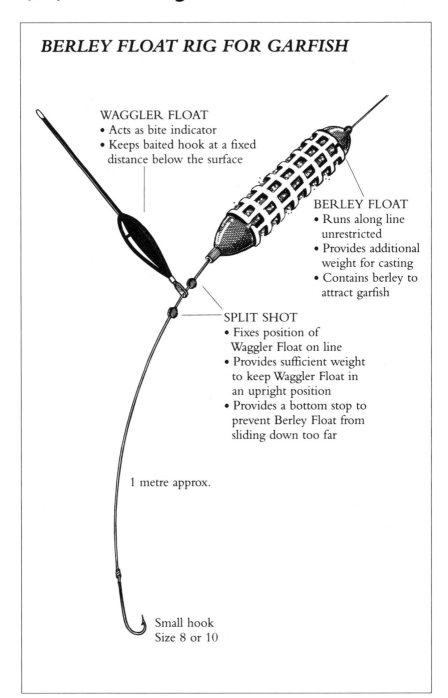

WAGGLER FLOAT
• Acts as bite indicator
• Keeps baited hook at a fixed
distance below the surface

BERLEY FLOAT
• Runs along line
unrestricted
• Provides additional
weight for casting
• Contains berley to
attract garfish

SPLIT SHOT
• Fixes position of
Waggler Float on line
• Provides sufficient weight
to keep Waggler Float in
an upright position
• Provides a bottom stop to
prevent Berley Float from
sliding down too far

1 metre approx.

Small hook
Size 8 or 10

BERLEY FEEDER RIG FOR FRESHWATER FISHING

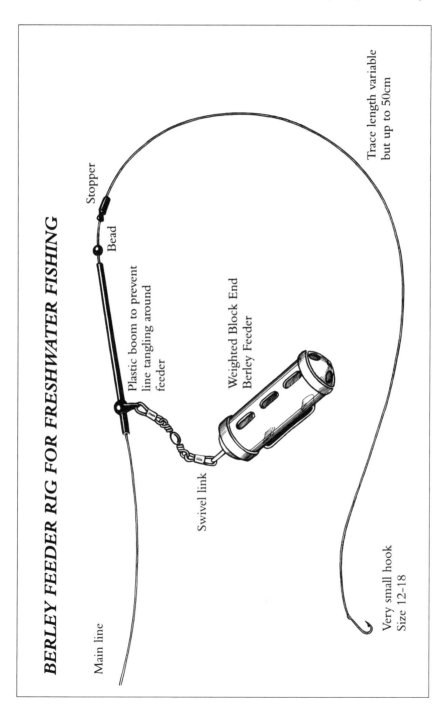

Main line

Stopper

Bead

Plastic boom to prevent line tangling around feeder

Weighted Block End Berley Feeder

Swivel link

Trace length variable but up to 50cm

Very small hook Size 12–18

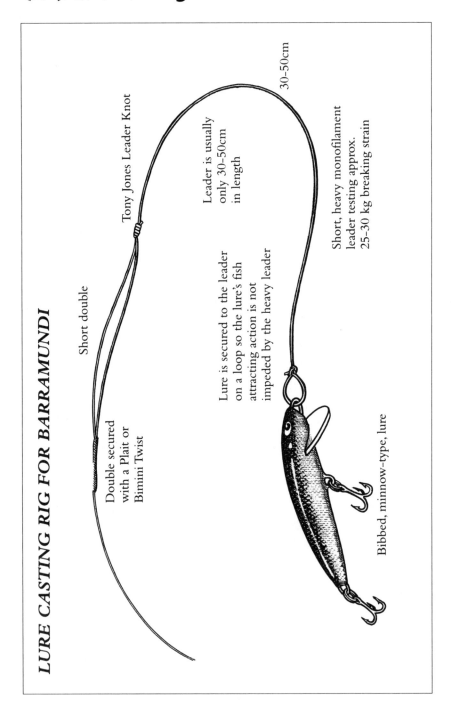

LURE CASTING RIG FOR BARRAMUNDI

Short double

Tony Jones Leader Knot

30–50cm

Leader is usually only 30–50cm in length

Short, heavy monofilament leader testing approx. 25–30 kg breaking strain

Double secured with a Plait or Bimini Twist

Lure is secured to the leader on a loop so the lure's fish attracting action is not impeded by the heavy leader

Bibbed, minnow-type, lure

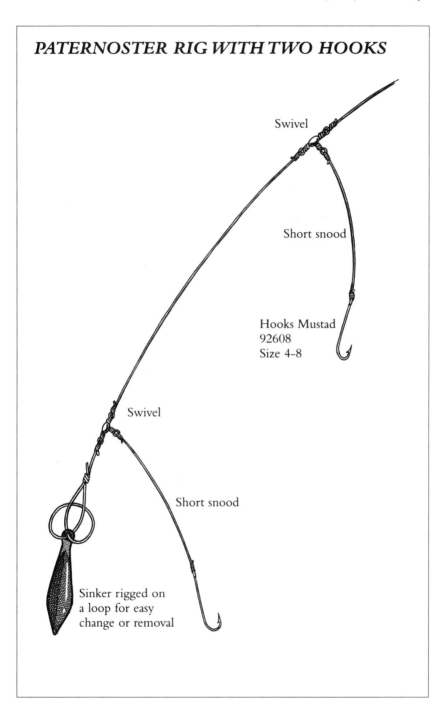

PATERNOSTER RIG WITH TWO HOOKS

Swivel

Short snood

Hooks Mustad
92608
Size 4-8

Swivel

Short snood

Sinker rigged on
a loop for easy
change or removal

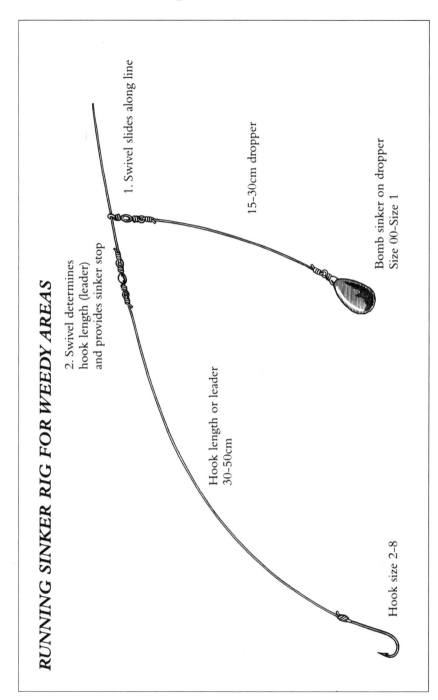

RUNNING SINKER RIG FOR WEEDY AREAS

1. Swivel slides along line

2. Swivel determines hook length (leader) and provides sinker stop

15–30cm dropper

Bomb sinker on dropper
Size 00–Size 1

Hook length or leader
30–50cm

Hook size 2–8

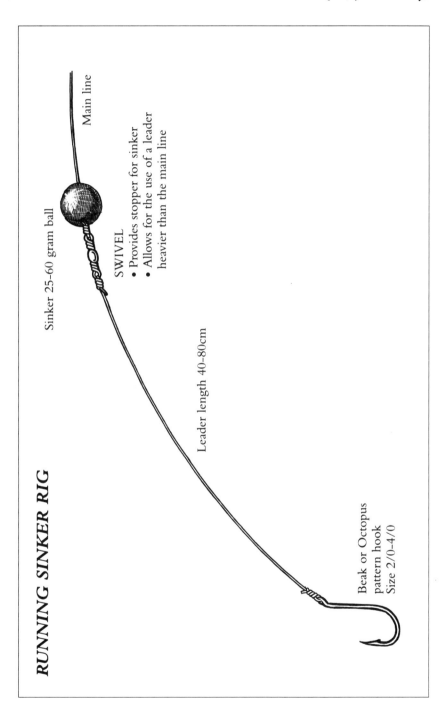

RUNNING SINKER RIG

Main line

Sinker 25-60 gram ball

SWIVEL
• Provides stopper for sinker
• Allows for the use of a leader heavier than the main line

Leader length 40-80cm

Beak or Octopus pattern hook
Size 2/0-4/0

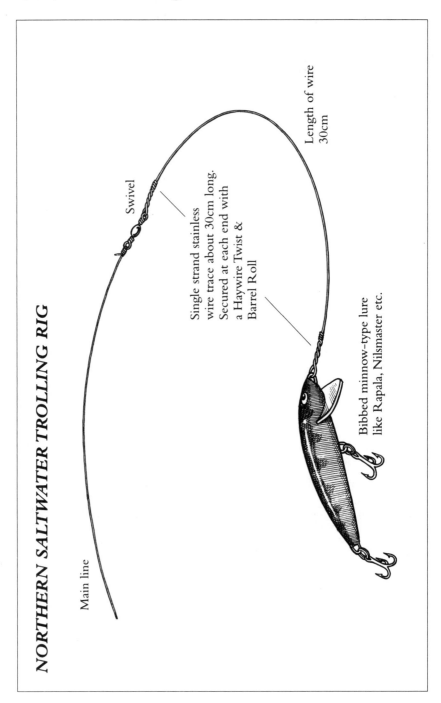

NORTHERN SALTWATER TROLLING RIG

Main line

Swivel

Single strand stainless wire trace about 30cm long. Secured at each end with a Haywire Twist & Barrel Roll

Length of wire 30cm

Bibbed minnow-type lure like Rapala, Nilsmaster etc.

OFFSHORE TROLLING RIG FOR GAME FISH

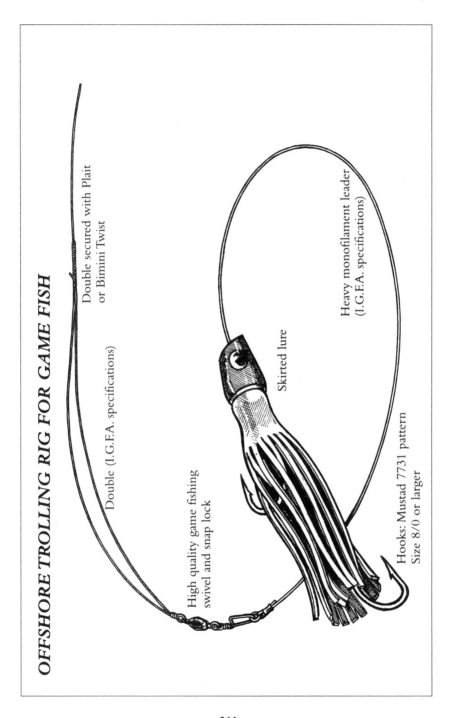

Double secured with Plait or Bimini Twist

Double (I.G.F.A. specifications)

Heavy monofilament leader (I.G.F.A. specifications)

Skirted lure

High quality game fishing swivel and snap lock

Hooks: Mustad 7731 pattern Size 8/0 or larger

Fishing Diary

WHERE:

DATE:

TIME:

WEATHER:

TIDE:

BAROMETER:

WIND:

The Fish

SPECIES:

WEIGHT:

BAIT USED:

OTHER DETAILS:

Fishing Diary

WHERE:

DATE:

TIME:

WEATHER:

TIDE:

BAROMETER:

WIND:

The Fish

SPECIES:

WEIGHT:

BAIT USED:

OTHER DETAILS:

Fishing Diary

WHERE:

DATE:

TIME:

WEATHER:

TIDE:

BAROMETER:

WIND:

The Fish

SPECIES:

WEIGHT:

BAIT USED:

OTHER DETAILS:

Fishing Diary

WHERE:

DATE:

TIME:

WEATHER:

TIDE:

BAROMETER:

WIND:

The Fish

SPECIES:

WEIGHT:

BAIT USED:

OTHER DETAILS:

Fishing Diary

WHERE:

DATE:

TIME:

WEATHER:

TIDE:

BAROMETER:

WIND:

The Fish

SPECIES:

WEIGHT:

BAIT USED:

OTHER DETAILS:

Fishing Diary

WHERE:

DATE:

TIME:

WEATHER:

TIDE:

BAROMETER:

WIND:

The Fish

SPECIES:

WEIGHT:

BAIT USED:

OTHER DETAILS:

Fishing Diary

WHERE:

DATE:

TIME:

WEATHER:

TIDE:

BAROMETER:

WIND:

The Fish

SPECIES:

WEIGHT:

BAIT USED:

OTHER DETAILS:

Fishing Diary

WHERE:

DATE:

TIME:

WEATHER:

TIDE:

BAROMETER:

WIND:

The Fish

SPECIES:

WEIGHT:

BAIT USED:

OTHER DETAILS:

Fishing Diary

WHERE:

DATE:

TIME:

WEATHER:

TIDE:

BAROMETER:

WIND:

The Fish

SPECIES:

WEIGHT:

BAIT USED:

OTHER DETAILS:

Fishing Diary

WHERE:

DATE:

TIME:

WEATHER:

TIDE:

BAROMETER:

WIND:

The Fish

SPECIES:

WEIGHT:

BAIT USED:

OTHER DETAILS:

Fishing Diary

WHERE:

DATE:

TIME:

WEATHER:

TIDE:

BAROMETER:

WIND:

The Fish

SPECIES:

WEIGHT:

BAIT USED:

OTHER DETAILS:

Yibbida Yibbida
That's all folks!